Everybody's
Business
Scoreboard

Corporate America's Winners, Losers, and Also-Rans

Edited by
Milton Moskowitz
Michael Katz
Robert Levering

1817

HARPER & ROW, PUBLISHERS, SAN FRANCISCO

Cambridge, Hagerstown, Philadelphia, New York,
London, Mexico City, São Paulo, Sydney

Acknowledgments

This book reflects the strength of American business publishing. Of primary importance to us was the work done by *Advertising Age,* as perceptive and accurate a trade publication as you will find anywhere. Our researcher was Marilee Strong, a journalist with curiosity and tenacity. Two other journalists, Susan Shepard and Carol Townsend, made important contributions.

FIRST EDITION

Charts and Graphs by
Richard Leon and James Carruth
Drawings by David Broad

Library of Congress Cataloging in Publication Data
Main entry under title:

Everybody's business scoreboard.

    1. Corporations—United States—Handbooks, manuals, etc. 2. Big business—United States— Handbook, manuals, etc. 3. United States— Commerce—Handbooks, manuals, etc. 4. United States—Industries—Handbooks, manuals, etc. I. Moskowitz, Milton. II. Katz, Michael. III. Levering, Robert.
HD2785.E89   1983   338.7′4′0973   82-48420
ISBN 0-06-250626-9

---

83 84 85 86 87 10 9 8 7 6 5 4 3 2 1

Contents*

*The items under each chapter title represent only a partial list of what you'll find in the book.

V. We'll Buy It and Put a Hotel on It

America's Biggest Mergers . . . Corporate Incest . . . Beatrice Foods' Big Arms . . . The 10 Most Active Corporate Acquirers . . . Most Rapacious Companies in America . . . If You Can't Beat 'em, Join 'em . . . Who Says Affirmative Action Doesn't Work? . . . Tops in Slots . . . Where America Sleeps . . . When to Speculate . . . Nation's Top 10 Law Firms . . . Don't Tackle a Big Company Unless You Have a Lot of Money for Lawyers . . .

VI. The One Place Where the U.S. Is Still Supreme (God Help Us): Advertising

Does Anyone Want to Move to Portugal? . . . Vice-Presidential Mania . . . Top U.S. Ad Agencies . . . America's Biggest Advertisers . . . Most Expensive Piece of White Space Around . . . God is Like . . . What It Costs to Buy a Page of Advertising . . . Milestones in American Culture . . . The Richest People in America . . . Flacks, Keep Out . . . Most Watched TV Shows of All Time . . . What America Reads . . . Englishmen Don't Read Magazines . . .

VII. So This Is the Way the World Ends

Everybody's Wired in Palm Springs . . . Triumph of Chemistry over Nature . . . Top Cigarette and Liquor Brands . . . America's Real Growth Industry: Health Care . . . Companies Paying No Federal Income Taxes . . . What the Future Looks Like . . . Who Makes the Bomb? . . .

Where to Find It

I/Welcome to the World of Business

Portrait of the Average American

—Consumes 374 beers and 92 hot dogs a year
—Eats 310 hogs and 26 acres of grain by age 70
—In a lifetime piles up garbage 600 to 700 times
  his or her weight

Source: *Journal of American Insurance.*

Most Successful New Products of the Past 10 Years

Tostitos	$160 million a year for a cracker
Pac-Man	A billion-dollar business overnight
Miller Lite	Became one of top four beer brands on long series of memorable commercials
"Star Wars"	No movie has ever taken in more money: more than $1 billion at box office
Walkman	Sony has sold 4½ million since 1979
Toyota Corolla	Now the world's top-selling car
Tagamet	SmithKline's anti-ulcer drug displaced Valium as top prescription seller

The Healthy American

Annual Adult Intake:

—3,850 cigarettes
—2 gallons of wine
—24½ gallons of beer
—39½ gallons of soft drinks
—1.98 gallons of liquor

TV Junkies

The average American spends more time in front of the TV set than at work: 50 hours a week.

The Competitive U.S. Marketplace

Soups: Campbell owns 80% of the business.

Color Film: Kodak has 85% of the market.

Disposable Diapers: Procter & Gamble (Pampers and Luvs) has a 70%-plus share.

Most Misleading Company Names

Standard Oil of California (*main crude oil source: Saudi Arabia*)

Dart & Kraft (*sounds like a toy company*)

Gulf & Western Industries (*headquartered off Central Park in New York*)

Continental Group (*they make cans*)

Norton Simon (*Norton Simon himself is not even on the board anymore*)

Greyhound (*biggest business: Armour meats*)

Worst Business Decisions

Du Pont's acquisition of Conoco

U.S. Steel's acquisition of Marathon Oil

Exxon's acquisition of Reliance Electric

Atlantic Richfield's acquisition of Anaconda

Procter & Gamble's Rely tampons

Ford's placement of the Pinto gas tank

General Motors' spying on Ralph Nader

Tenglemann's purchase of 50% of A&P chain

Renault's acquisition of controlling interest in American Motors

Volkswagen's building the Rabbit in Pennsylvania

Mobil's purchase of Montgomery Ward

Schlitz's reformulation of its beer

Sambo's revamping of profit-sharing formula with restaurant managers

Land O' Lakes introduction of margarine

Pan Am's purchase of National Airlines

United Artists' bankrolling of *Heaven's Gate*

The 25 Largest Corporate Employers

1.	AT&T	1,042,000
2.	GENERAL MOTORS	740,000
3.	GENERAL ELECTRIC	404,000
4.	FORD MOTOR	404,000
5.	SEARS, ROEBUCK	395,000
6.	IBM	348,000
7.	ITT	336,000
8.	K MART	268,000
9.	MOBIL	209,000
10.	GENERAL TELEPHONE & ELECTRONICS	202,000
11.	F. W. WOOLWORTH	198,000
12.	UNITED TECHNOLOGIES	195,000
13.	J. C. PENNEY	193,000
14.	EXXON	180,000
15.	DU PONT	156,000
16.	SAFEWAY	153,000
17.	WESTINGHOUSE	147,000
18.	U.S. STEEL	141,000
19.	GOODYEAR TIRE	138,000
20.	RCA	126,000
21.	MCDONALD'S	126,000
22.	GULF & WESTERN	122,000
23.	XEROX	120,000
24.	PEPSICO	120,000
25.	FEDERATED DEPARTMENT STORES	118,000

Who Pays for Health Care

In 1965, when health care costs were $41.7 billion, patients themselves paid for slightly more than half those costs. In 1981, when health care costs were $286.6 billion, two-thirds were borne by "third parties" such as Blue Cross and Blue Shield, Medicare and Medicaid, and private health insurers.

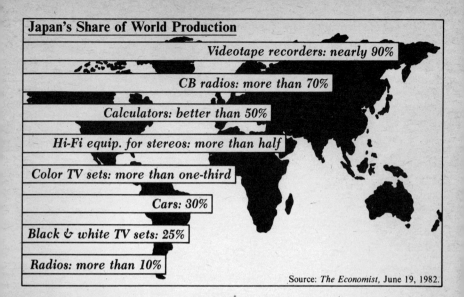

Japan's Share of World Production

Videotape recorders: nearly 90%

CB radios: more than 70%

Calculators: better than 50%

Hi-Fi equip. for stereos: more than half

Color TV sets: more than one-third

Cars: 30%

Black & white TV sets: 25%

Radios: more than 10%

Source: *The Economist*, June 19, 1982.

Geniuses at Work

Some new products tested by companies in 1981 were:

Tidal Wave Bubble Gum (*Wm. Wrigley, Jr.*)

Active Liquid Yogurt (*Coca-Cola*)

Headway Cold Medicine (*Richardson-Vicks*)

Surround Cough Syrup (*Richardson-Vicks*)

Post Wishing Stars Cereal (*General Foods*)

Coffee Velvet Flavoring (*Dart & Kraft*)

Le Culteur Yogurt Drink Mix (*Fillmore Foods*)

Lil' Salt Bologna (*Zemco Industries*)

Mickey Mouse Lunchbags (*Carrousel Products*)

Tap-a-Drop Deodorizer (*Nil-Odor*)

Caffeine-Free Sunkist (*General Cinema*)

Night Glories Makeup (*Squibb*)

Maximum Cramp Relief Pamprin (*Chattem Labs*)

One Big Happy Family

H. J. Heinz

Heinz ketchup
Star-Kist tuna
Weight Watchers

The Only Head of a Major Company Who Was Born in Poland

Arthur B. Belfer, founder and chairman of Belco Petroleum, New York–headquartered oil producer whose major fields are in Peru

3

Business Publications: The Big Four

	FREQUENCY	CIRCULATION	COST OF FULL-PAGE AD
The Wall Street Journal (*Dow Jones & Co.*)	Every weekday	2,000,000	$56,000
BusinessWeek (*McGraw-Hill*)	Weekly	777,000	$21,000
Forbes (*Forbes Inc.*)	Every other week	700,000	$16,500
Fortune (*Time Inc.*)	Every other week	674,000	$20,000

40-and-Under Club

AGE IN 1982	HEAD OF COMPANY	COMPANY
37	Frederick W. Smith	Federal Express
38	Charles A. Vose, Jr.	First Oklahoma Bancorp
38	Arthur D. Little	Narragansett Capital
39	Joseph R. Hyde III	Malone & Hyde
39	Irwin L. Jacobs	Jacobs Industries
40	A. C. Markkula, Jr.	Apple Computer
40	Michael D. Rose	Holiday Inns
40	Peter A. Magowan	Safeway Stores
40	B. Gill Clements	SEDCO
40	Finn M. W. Caspersen	Beneficial Finance
40	Edward P. Evans	Macmillan

The Over-75 Club

AGE IN 1982	COMPANY CHAIRMAN	COMPANY
84	Armand Hammer	Occidental Petroleum
83	Earle M. Jorgensen	Earle M. Jorgensen Co.
80	S. Mark Taper	First Charter Financial
78	Dean A. McGee	Kerr-McGee
77	John F. Connelly	Crown Cork & Seal
76	Leonard H. Goldenson	American Broadcasting Companies
75	Arthur B. Belfer	Belco Petroleum
75	H. Everett Olson	Carnation

A Checkered Past

The last Checker taxicab rolled off the assembly line at Kalamazoo, Michigan, on July 12, 1982.

The Dozen Oldest Companies in America

1702   **J. E. Rhoads & Sons,** Philadelphia. Leather belting, tanners. Oldest company of any kind operating continuously. Now in Newark, Delaware, where a ninth generation family member works under the supervision of an eighth generation relative.

1728   **The Saturday Evening Post** magazine, founded in Philadelphia, now out of Indianapolis. Has undergone several renaissances. For the first 200 years or so, issues appeared regularly, except during the American Revolution when the British occupied Philadelphia and when the publisher was with the Continental Congress.

1743   **Skillman Express, Storage & Furniture Exchange,** Princeton, New Jersey. Now run by a stepson of a descendant of Thomas Skillman, founder.

1752   **Caswell-Massey Co., Ltd.,** New York. Druggists, perfumists. Believed to be the oldest chemists in America. Pharmacy is on Manhattan's East Side.

1754   **Devoe & Raynolds Co., Inc.,** Louisville, Kentucky. America's oldest paint manufacturer, now part of the Grow Group.

1760   **P. Lorillard,** New York. America's oldest tobacco manufacturer, now part of Loews Corporation, theatres and hotels.

1764   **Hartford Courant,** Hartford, Connecticut. Daily newspaper. Oldest paper of continuous publication in the country.

1766   **Gladding's,** Providence, Rhode Island. America's oldest women's specialty clothing store. Closed briefly, but brought back to life by Johnson & Wales College of Providence.

1767   **C. H. Dexter & Sons,** now **Dexter Corp.** of Windsor Locks, Connecticut. Specialty paper products. Oldest company on the New York Stock Exchange and still run by a descendant (David Coffin) of the founding family on the original location.

1770   **Demuth Tobacco Shop,** Lancaster, Pennsylvania. Oldest tobacco shop in America, operating on original site by descendants of the founder, a fifth generation family member.

1775   **Bowne & Co.,** New York. Financial printers. Oldest company on the American Stock Exchange and believed to be the oldest in New York operating under the same name since its inception.

1776   **Kirk & Nice,** Philadelphia. Funeral directors. Germantown's oldest business enterprise, still operated by descendants of the original founding family.

Source: Etna Kelley, *Business Founding Date Directory* (New York: Etna Kelley).

Companies That Gave Up the Business They Started With

	ORIGINAL BUSINESS		ORIGINAL BUSINESS
Scovill	Brass	Penn Central	Railroading
Allegheny International	Steel	Textron	Textiles
Northwest Industries	Railroading	Ronson	Cigarette lighters
Dart & Kraft	Rexall drugstores (Dart)	Jewel Companies	Home food delivery
Wm. Wrigley Jr.	Soap	Resorts International	Paints
Chris-Craft Industries	Boats	General Host	Bread
Outlet Company	Stores	Warner Communications	Funeral homes
Interstate Bakeries	Computer leasing	W. R. Grace	Shipping
Charter Company	Lumber	Mickelberry	Meat processing

The Company with the Biggest Financial Loss in History
Chrysler lost $1.7 billion in 1980 (please buy one of their cars)

The Company with the Biggest Profit in the History of Business
AT&T or Ma Bell, $6.9 billion in 1981 (no wonder they're being split up)

The Company with the Greatest Increase in Charitable Contributions
Standard Oil of California (quadrupled since 1978 to $20 million; they must have a guilty conscience)

The Company with More Women Officers Than Anyone Else (55)
Equitable Life Assurance

The Nation's Largest Employer of Blacks
AT&T (more than 100,000)

Foot-in-the-Mouth Award

To J. Peter Grace, chairman of the W. R. Grace conglomerate, one of whose arms is the Del Taco fast-food Mexican chain, who went to work to help Ronald Reagan reduce government spending. In a talk before the American Feed and Grain Manufacturers Association, Grace dismissed the federal food-stamp program as "basically a Puerto Rican program." Grace said 900,000 Puerto Ricans "live in New York and they're all on food stamps." Grace was paid $2.3 million in 1981.

How Good the Air Smells

Americans are spending a lot of money to drive the bad smells away. According to Packaged Facts, a New York–based research company, annual spending is now $230 million for air fresheners; $175 million for electronic air cleaners; $100 million for carpet fresheners; $35 million for toilet bowl fresheners; and $15 million for home fragrances.

The Pet Business

The Market

49 million dogs
42 million cats
25 million birds
250 million other household pets

What's Spent Annually

$4.3 billion for pet foods
$760 million for equipment (aquariums, litter boxes, leashes)
$700 million for purchase of pets
$420 million for services (kennels, grooming)
$350 million for health and grooming aids (vitamins, flea powders, combs)
$1.6 billion for veterinarians (the U.S. has 24,000 vets)

Result: an $8 billion-a-year market

Sources: Pet Food Institute; American Pet Products Manufacturers Association.

The Big Corporate Dog and Cat Feeders

	1981 Sales	Share
Ralston Purina (*Dog Chow, Cat Chow, Tender Vittles*)	$1.2 *billion*	28.5%
Carnation (*Mighty Dog, Friskies*)	$480 *million*	11%
General Foods (*Gravy Train, Gainesburgers*)	$390 *million*	8.8%
Quaker Oats (*Ken-L-Ration, Tender Chunks*)	$340 *million*	7.8%
Liggett (*Alpo*)	$240 *million*	5.5%
All others	$1.7 *billion*	38.4%
Total	$4.3 billion	100%

Source: *Advertising Age,* May 10, 1982. John C. Maxwell.

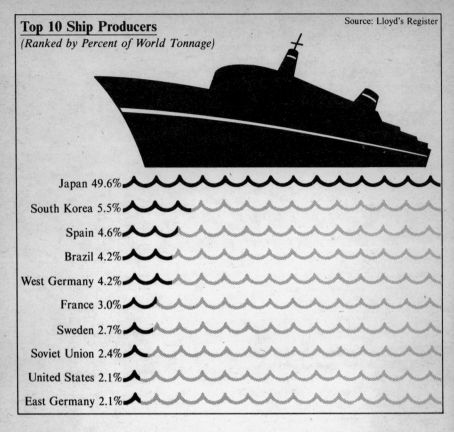

Top 10 Ship Producers
(Ranked by Percent of World Tonnage)

Source: Lloyd's Register

Japan 49.6%
South Korea 5.5%
Spain 4.6%
Brazil 4.2%
West Germany 4.2%
France 3.0%
Sweden 2.7%
Soviet Union 2.4%
United States 2.1%
East Germany 2.1%

The Rise of the German Chemists:
The Six Largest Chemical Companies (by Sales)

1970

1. **DuPont** (*U.S.*)	$3.6 *billion*
2. **ICI** (*Britain*)	$3.5 *billion*
3. **Hoechst** (*West Germany*)	$3.0 *billion*
4. **Union Carbide** (*U.S.*)	$3.0 *billion*
5. **BASF** (*West Germany*)	$2.9 *billion*
6. **Montedison** (*Italy*)	$2.8 *billion*

1980

1. **Hoechst** (*West Germany*)	$16.5 *billion*
2. **Bayer** (*West Germany*)	$15.9 *billion*
3. **BASF** (*West Germany*)	$15.3 *billion*
4. **DuPont** (*U.S.*)	$13.7 *billion*
5. **ICI** (*Britain*)	$13.3 *billion*
6. **Dow Chemical** (*U.S.*)	$10.6 *billion*

Steel Away: The Top Steel Producers

1. Nippon Steel (Japan)
2. U.S. Steel (U.S.)
3. NKK (Japan)
4. Finsider (Italy)
5. Bethlehem Steel (U.S.)
6. Thyssen (Germany)
7. Sumitomo (Japan)
8. Kawasaki (Japan)
9. Arbed (Luxembourg)
10. Usinor (France)

Source: *Financial Times*, August 17, 1981.

The Pause That Refreshes
Coca-Cola Advertising Themes Through the Ages

1886	Drink Coca-Cola
1904	Delicious and Refreshing
1905	Coca-Cola Revives and Sustains
1906	The Great National Temperance Beverage
1917	Three Million a Day
1922	Thirst Knows No Season
1925	Six Million a Day
1927	Around the Corner from Everywhere
1929	The Pause That Refreshes
1932	Ice Cold Sunshine
1938	The Best Friend Thirst Ever Had
1939	Coca-Cola Goes Along, Wherever You Are, Whatever You Do, Wherever You May Be, When You Think of Refreshment Think of Ice Cold Coca-Cola
1942	The Only Thing Like Coca-Cola Is Coca-Cola Itself. It's the Real Thing.
1948	Where There's Coke There's Hospitality
1949	Coca-Cola: Along the Highway to Anywhere
1952	What You Want Is a Coke
1956	Coca-Cola Makes Good Things Taste Better
1957	Sign of Good Taste
1958	The Cold, Crisp Taste of Coke
1959	Be Really Refreshed
1963	Things Go Better with Coke
1970	It's the Real Thing
1971	I'd Like to Buy the World a Coke
1975	Look Up, America
1976	Coke Adds Life
1979	Have a Coke and a Smile
1982	Coke Is It

One Big Happy Family
Esmark

Swift meats
Playtex bras
Danskin tights
STP oil additive
Peter Pan peanut butter
Jensen speakers

In Case You Thought These Were American Companies

U.S. COMPANY	REAL OWNER
1. Shell Oil (*Houston*) *Fourth largest seller of gasoline in the U.S.*	69%-owned by Royal Dutch/Shell Group, an Anglo-Dutch hybrid.
2. Joseph E. Seagram & Sons (*New York*) *Top-ranking wine and liquor producer (Paul Masson, Chivas Regal, V.O., 7 Crown, Mumm's, and on and on).*	Canada's Seagram company.
3. Standard Oil of Ohio (*Cleveland*) *SOHIO is the second largest producer of oil from U.S. fields (mostly Alaskan).*	53%-owned by British Petroleum, whose major shareholders are the British government (22%) and the Bank of England (17%).
4. Great Atlantic & Pacific Tea Co. (*Montvale, New Jersey*) *A&P is the fourth largest U.S. supermarket chain.*	50%-owned by Germany's Tengelmann Group.
5. North American Philips (*New York*) *Biggest electric shaver maker (Norelco), also markets TV sets and other electronic products under Magnavox, Sylvania, and Philco names.*	62%-owned by a trust set up by Philips of the Netherlands, one of the giants of the world's electronics industry.
6. BATUS (*Louisville*). *Third largest U.S. cigarette maker (Viceroy, Kool, Raleigh, Barclay), also owner of Saks Fifth Avenue, Gimbel's, Marshall Field, and Kohl's.*	B.A.T Industries, London, the world's largest cigarette maker (outside of government-owned entities).
7. Miles Laboratories (*Elkhart, Indiana*) *Maker of Alka-Seltzer, One-A-Day vitamins, S.O.S. soap pads, Bactine antiseptic.*	Germany's Bayer company, world's second largest chemical producer and the inventor of aspirin.
8. Lever Bros. (*New York*) *(Lux, Dove, All, Close-up, Wisk, Imperial)* *Thomas J. Lipton, Englewood Cliffs, New Jersey (Lipton teas and instant soups, Wishbone salad dressings, Good Humor ice cream).*	Unilever, another Anglo-Dutch (London and Rotterdam) hybrid, the eleventh largest company in the world outside the U.S.
9. Crocker National (*San Francisco*) *Thirteenth largest commercial bank in the U.S.*	54%-owned by Midland Bank, London, largest commercial bank in the United Kingdom.
10. American Motors (*Southfield, Michigan*) *Fourth ranking U.S. auto maker.*	46%-owned by Renault, which is 100%-owned by the French government and Europe's largest auto maker.
11. Nestle (*White Plains, New York*) Stouffer (*Solon, Ohio*) Libby, McNeil & Libby (*Chicago*) Beech-Nut (*Ft. Washington, Pennsylvania*)	Nestle of Switzerland, world's largest packaged foods manufacturer.
12. Marine Midland (*Buffalo, New York*) *Fourteenth largest bank in the U.S.*	51%-owned by Hongkong & Shanghai Banking of Hong Kong.
13. Liggett Group (*Montvale, New Jersey*) *Sixth largest U.S. cigarette maker (L&M, Chesterfield, Lark, Eve, generic no-names), has No. 1 canned dog food (Alpo), markets long line of imported wines and liquors (J&B Scotch, Bailey's Original Irish Cream, Grand Marnier, Bombay gin).*	Grand Metropolitan, London, a giant hotel, dairy, restaurant, gambling and beverage conglomerate (relieved Pan Am of Intercontinental Hotels in 1981).

14. McDonough (*Parkersburg, West Virginia*)
   (*Endicott Johnson and Nettleton shoes, Liberty shoe stores, Father & Son shoe stores, Merit shoe stores*).
   Hygrade Food Products (*Southfield, Michigan*)
   Hygrade hot dogs.
   Interstate United (*Chicago*)
   Major vending machine operator and manager of restaurants in schools and factories.

   Hanson Trust, London, British conglomerate with interests here, there and everywhere (earth-moving equipment, flour miller, photo labs, pumps, twines, trade magazines, printing, yarns, textile machinery).

15. Howard Johnson (*Braintree, Massachusetts*)
   Major restaurant and motel operator.

   Imperial Group, Britain's largest cigarette manufacturer.

16. Hoffmann-La Roche (*Nutley, New Jersey*)
   Major pharmaceutical and vitamin producer (developer of Valium).

   F. Hoffmann-LaRoche of Switzerland.

17. Beecham Group (*Clifton, New Jersey*)
   Medicine chest full of Brylcreem, Yardley, Jovan musk oil, Aqua-fresh toothpaste, Calgon bath oil beads, Massengil douches, Hold cough drops.

   Beecham Group, London, major drug and toiletries producer.

18. Spiegel (*Chicago*)
   Mail order house.

   Otto Versand of Germany.

19. Timex (*Waterbury, Connecticut*)
   Major watch producer.

   Olsen and Lehmkuhl families of Norway.

20. Bic Pen (*Milford, Connecticut*)
   No. 1 ballpoint pen producer, also battles Gillette in disposable lighters and disposable razors.

   57%-owned by the Bic company of France.

Jobs Lost Due to Auto Imports: An American View

Industry Week published a study that claimed that more than 400,000 Americans lost their jobs in 1981 because of foreign car imports. Below is a summary of which workers lost their jobs:

Automotive Workers	131,909
Raw Materials Suppliers	72,664
Parts Suppliers	52,815
Plant Machinery Makers	38,689
Retailers and Restaurants	38,434
Wholesalers	37,409
Office, Advertising, etc.	23,407
Transporters	19,682
Miscellaneous	27,991
Total Jobs Lost	443,000

Source: *Industry Week*, June 14, 1982.

Jobs Gained from Auto Imports: A Japanese View

Toyota counters charges that auto imports cost Americans jobs by pointing to their investments in the U.S. ($1.2 billion), their annual expenditures here ($1.6 billion for payroll and American-made goods and services), and the jobs Toyota provides for Americans:

Dealerships	31,145
Toyota U.S.A.	1,958
Longshoremen, etc.	1,809
Independent Distributors	929
Jobs Gained from Toyota	35,841
Jobs Gained from All Imports	150,000*

* Toyota's estimate.

Where Tycoons Come From

Etymology

Venture:	close to original meaning of "pirate"
Tycoon:	title of Japanese warlords of 19th century
Mogul:	derived from the Mongols
Colossus:	derived from the Greek "kolossos," meaning gigantic statue
Titan:	term for "sons of Heaven"; their early leader, Kronos, did a "fearful deed," castrating his father, Heaven; Zeus eventually overthrew the Titans
Well-heeled:	comes from cockfighting, where cocks were armed with metal heels to enable them to use their feet as swords

Source: Steele Commager in March 29, 1982, *Forbes*.

Language of Business: Insurance

A policyholder who was insured for disability had his disability payments reduced after he started to receive disability benefits from Social Security. He wrote to the company that had insured him, Old Republic Life Insurance of Chicago, to inquire about this reduction. Back came this one-sentence reply:

The contract stipulates if the total monthly amount of loss of time benefits promised for the same loss under all valid loss of time coverage upon the insured person, whether payable on a weekly or monthly basis shall exceed the monthly earnings of the insured person at the time disability commenced or his average monthly earnings for the period of two years immediately proceeding [sic] a disability for which claim is made, which ever is greater, the Company will be liable only for such portion and amount of such benefits under the certificate as the amount of such monthly earnings or such monthly earnings of the insured person bears to the total amount of monthly benefits with the same loss under all such coverage upon the insured person at the time of such disability commences and for the return of such part of the premiums paid during such two years as shall exceed the pro-rated amount of premiums for the benefits and repaid hereunder but this shall no [sic] operate the reduced total monthly amount of benefits payable under all such coverage upon the insured person below the sum of $200.00, or the sum of the monthly benefits specified in such coverage, which ever is the lesser nor shall it operate to reduce benefits other then [sic] those payable for loss of time.

The $22.5 Million Paycheck

Steven J. Ross took more money out of Warner Communications in 1981 than has ever been taken out of any U.S. corporation in one year by any chief executive officer, including all the past and present heads of IBM, General Motors, and Exxon.

How did Ross collect his $22.5 million? Warner certainly didn't pay him $432,692 a week or $10,817.30 an hour.

For openers, Warner's chairman had an annual salary of $350,000. His employment contract also grants him a bonus equal to five-eighths of one percent of Warner's aftertax profits. In 1981 that was good for another $1.6 million.

Next, Warner provided Ross with a car, helped him with his taxes, and bought a lot of life insurance for him. Those benefits totalled $72,000. On top of that, Ross received $1.1 million of contingent pay—partly a bonus based on earnings growth, partly deferred compensation (money banked for his retirement).

That's $3 million so far. What about the other $19 million? You have to look closely at the proxy statement sent to all shareholders to figure that out.

The proxy explains carefully that in 1977 Ross was granted 150,000 bonus units, which grew to 533,332 bonus units after subsequent stock splits. (A Bonus Unit is a payout based on increases in the price of the company's stock.) When Ross received these units, the price was pegged at $7.59 a share. Warner's stock skyrocketed after the acquisition of Atari, maker of Space Invaders and Pac Man video games, to over $50 a share. In 1981 Ross cashed in his 1977 bonus units for $12.5 million.

The remaining $7 million? This was apparently realized through a complicated stock transaction. Instead of selling 360,000 shares of stock he had held for a number of years, Ross sold the same number of shares he had acquired by exercising stock options during the previous three years. This saved Warner a lot of money on its taxes, but stuck Ross with a lethal tax bite on a short-term gain. So Warner paid him $1.8 million to cover the extra tax bite.

The result: Ross got his money and Warner was able to save $4 million on its tax bill. Everyone came out ahead, except for the IRS.

Vintage Year for Red Ink

Car Companies, Airlines, Savings and Loans, Supermarkets, Breweries—You Name It, They Lost Money in 1981

LOSS IN 1981

1. Ford Motor	$1,060,100,000	
2. Chrysler	$475,600,000	
3. Kaiser Steel	$437,455,000	
4. International Harvester	$393,128,000	
5. Lockheed	$311,600,000	
6. AM International	$245,051,000	
7. Commonwealth Oil Refining	$212,309,000	
8. Federal National Mortgage Association	$190,370,000	
9. Braniff International	$160,611,000	
10. American Motors	$136,563,000	
11. Combustion Equipment Associates	$129,944,000	
12. Coastal	$96,399,000	
13. Gulf Resources & Chemicals	$77,929,000	
14. United Airlines	$70,530,000	
15. Eastern Airlines	$65,877,000	
16. U.S. Industries	$62,671,000	
17. H. F. Ahmanson	$61,498,000	
18. Fidelity Financial	$56,940,000	
19. Envirotech	$55,987,000	
20. First Charter Financial	$55,654,000	
21. Gibraltar Financial Corp. of California	$54,188,000	
22. Cities Service	$49,200,000	
23. Equimark	$47,101,000	
24. Republic Airlines	$46,269,000	
25. Great Atlantic & Pacific Tea	$43,049,000	
26. McLouth Steel	$40,000,000	
27. Fiat-Allis	$39,975,000	
28. Imperial Corporation of America	$37,754,000	
29. Wilson Foods	$36,987,000	
30. Financial Federation	$32,024,000	
31. Financial Corporation of Santa Barbara	$30,166,000	
32. Allis-Chalmers	$28,841,000	
33. Great Western Financial	$28,159,000	
34. Bird & Son	$27,060,000	
35. Western Financial	$25,526,000	
36. DRE	$24,364,000	
37. Publicker Industries	$23,978,000	
38. Pabst Brewing	$23,536,000	
39. Colonial Penn Group	$23,158,000	
40. J. P. Stevens	$22,874,000	
41. Energy Reserves Group	$22,606,000	
42. Centran	$22,160,000	
43. Jos. Schlitz Brewing	$20,604,000	
44. Questor	$20,365,000	
45. Transohio Financial	$19,322,000	
46. Golden West Financial	$19,157,000	
47. Broadview Financial	$19,071,000	
48. General Refractors	$18,951,000	
49. Pan Am	$18,875,000	
50. Hoover	$18,778,000	
51. Continental Steel	$17,080,000	
52. Tiger International	$16,613,000	
53. Ideal Toy	$15,452,000	
54. Northern California Savings & Loan	$15,408,000	
55. Westmoreland Coal	$14,775,000	
56. Old Stone	$14,697,000	
57. Toro	$13,068,000	
58. Jonathan Logan	$11,989,000	
59. Beneficial Corportion	$11,600,000	
60. Lever Brothers	$11,500,000	
61. Instrument Systems	$11,407,000	
62. Certain Teed	$10,916,000	
63. De Tomaso Industries	$10,619,000	
64. Pantry Pride	$10,614,000	
65. Rath Packing	$9,582,000	
66. Lamson & Sessions	$8,995,000	
67. Recognition Equipment	$8,167,000	
68. TMC Industries	$8,019,000	
69. Bibb	$7,917,000	
70. American Bakeries	$7,690,000	
71. American Savings & Loan Assn. of Florida	$7,665,000	
72. Compugraphic	$6,662,000	
73. Salant	$6,508,000	
74. First Pennsylvania	$6,424,000	
75. APL	$6,347,000	
76. Munsingwear	$6,251,000	
77. Pirelli Cable	$6,033,000	
78. Fedders	$5,392,000	
79. Tomlinson Oil	$5,387,000	
80. Roblin Industries	$5,359,000	
81. Clow	$4,872,000	
82. Beker Industries	$4,856,000	
83. Scovill	$4,534,000	
84. Talley Industries	$4,304,000	
85. Sun Electric	$4,278,000	

II/The Fight for Market Share

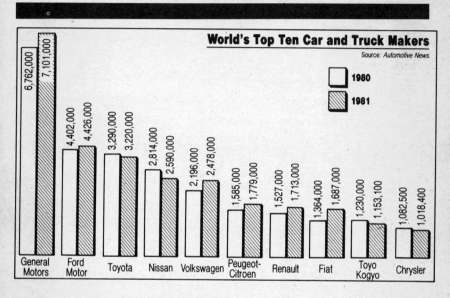

World's Top Ten Car and Truck Makers

Source: *Automotive News.*

- 1980
- 1981

Maker	1980	1981
General Motors	6,762,000	7,101,000
Ford Motor	4,402,000	4,426,000
Toyota	3,290,000	3,220,000
Nissan	2,814,000	2,590,000
Volkswagen	2,196,000	2,478,000
Peugeot-Citroen	1,585,000	1,779,000
Renault	1,527,000	1,713,000
Fiat	1,364,000	1,687,000
Toyo Kogyo	1,230,000	1,153,100
Chrysler	1,082,500	1,018,400

Detroit's Stake in Japanese Car Makers

Chrysler   Owns 15% of Mitsubishi Motors, Japan's fifth largest auto producer and builder of the Dodge Colt, Dodge Challenger, Plymouth Champ, and Plymouth Sapporo. Mitsubishi now exports its own line of cars to the U.S.: the Starion, Cordia, Tredia.

Ford   Owns 25% of Toyo Kogyo, Japan's fourth largest auto producer, maker of the Mazda. Toyo Kogyo builds the Courier minipickup for Ford.

General Motors   Owns 34% of Isuzu, Japan's seventh largest auto producer. Isuzu built the Opel for Buick and the Luv truck for Chevrolet. Now it sells its own line of cars and trucks in the U.S.

At Least It's No. 1 Somewhere

The largest maker and seller of automobiles in Mexico is Chrysler.

In a Sea of White Faces

The highest ranking black in corporate America is Otis M. Smith, vice-president and general counsel of General Motors.

General Motors has 11,100 car and truck dealers, of which 49 are black and 108 are members of other minority groups.

At the beginning of 1980 General Motors employed 625,800 workers; 19.2% (or 120,000) were minority group members. By June 1982 GM's U.S. employment was down to 492,000; 18.2% (or 90,000) were minority group members.

What's in a Name?

Top Car Sellers in 1981

BY NAMEPLATE

1. 346,307	CHEVETTE	34. 82,620	PONTIAC	67. 36,311	LEBARON (M)
2. 300,184	CITATION	35. 82,285	PHOENIX	68. 35,853	MAXIMA/810
3. 284,907	ESCORT	36. 82,263	LESABRE	69. 33,504	SPIRIT
4. 266,070	CUTLASS SUPREME	37. 77,980	DATSUN 310	70. 32,856	FIESTA
5. 241,603	TOYOTA COROLLA	38. 77,062	DATSUN 200SX	71. 32,825	TOYOTA STARLET
6. 211,130	MALIBU	39. 75,884	J2000/SUNBIRD	72. 31,902	BMW 320I
7. 210,424	CHEVROLET	40. 75,377	HORIZON	73. 29,733	MARK VI
8. 208,329	REGAL COUPE	41. 73,988	BONNEVILLE G/LEMANS	74. 29,583	TOYOTA CRESSIDA
9. 200,460	SKYLARK	42. 69,775	THUNDERBIRD	75. 29,178	LINCOLN
10. 196,997	RELIANT/VOLARE	43. 62,800	DATSUN 280ZX	76. 29,039	CORVETTE
11. 187,952	CUTLASS	44. 62,195	MAZDA GLC	77. 28,706	XR-7
12. 182,909	FAIRMONT	45. 60,475	MAZDA 626	78. 27,972	JETTA
13. 172,557	HONDA ACCORD	46. 59,846	CONCORD	79. 25,598	DIPLOMAT
14. 162,445	VW RABBIT	47. 57,234	ELECTRA	80. 23,904	CORDOBA
15. 161,158	MONTE CARLO	48. 56,038	OMNI	81. 22,724	SEVILLE
16. 159,939	DATSUN 210	49. 55,868	T1000	82. 22,337	TOYOTA CORONA
17. 158,662	OLDS 88	50. 54,502	EXP	83. 19,336	LE CAR
18. 154,985	MUSTANG	51. 54,389	ELDORADO	84. 18,368	VOLVO DL 4-DR.
19. 154,698	HONDA CIVIC	52. 53,145	MERCURY	85. 17,610	AUDI 5000
20. 152,062	SUBARU	53. 52,188	FIREBIRD	86. 17,080	CHRYSLER
21. 149,653	ARIES	54. 51,815	TC3	87. 17,043	VW SCIROCCO
22. 138,948	CADILLAC	55. 51,743	024	88. 16,292	MERCEDES 300SD
23. 128,236	GRAND PRIX	56. 50,603	ZEPHYR	89. 14,612	MERCEDES 2400
24. 123,676	REGAL SEDAN	57. 47,964	RIVIERA	90. 14,604	CIMARRON
25. 121,328	COROLLA TERCEL	58. 47,151	CAPRI	91. 13,947	MIRADA
26. 120,025	CELICA/SUPRA	59. 46,750	COUGAR	92. 13,688	MERCEDES 300D
27. 113,109	FORD	60. 43,450	HONDA PRELUDE	93. 13,634	AUDI 4000 4-E
28. 109,981	OMEGA	61. 43,418	MAZDA RX-7	94. 13,326	SAPPORO
29. 106,996	GRANADA	62. 43,221	EAGLE	95. 12,690	CHALLENGER
30. 94,606	CAMARO	63. 42,796	DODGE COLT	96. 12,081	RABBIT CONVERTIBLE
31. 92,809	LYNX	64. 42,128	PLYMOUTH CHAMP	97. 11,852	DASHER DIESEL
32. 88,072	CAVALIER/MONZA	65. 38,609	TORONADO	98. 11,570	FIAT SPIDER
33. 84,583	OLDS 98	66. 37,558	DATSUN 510	99. 11,561	VOLVO DL WAGON

Best Years for New Car Sales

Will We Ever Beat 1973 (The Year Before OPEC Struck)? Here were the best years for new car sales, ranked in order of number of passenger cars sold (including imports):

1973	11,350,995	1976	9,751,485	1974	8,701,094	1982	7,770,000	1959	6,041,275
1978	10,946,104	1969	9,446,524	1981	8,443,919	1963	7,556,717	1957	5,982,342
1977	10,826,234	1968	9,403,862	1970	8,388,204	1955	7,169,908	1956	5,955,248
1972	10,487,794	1965	9,313,912	1967	8,357,421	1962	6,938,863	1961	5,854,747
1979	10,356,695	1966	9,008,488	1975	8,261,840	1960	6,576,650	1953	5,738,989
1971	9,830,626	1980	8,760,937	1964	8,065,150	1950	6,326,438		

* Estimate.   Source: *Automotive News*, 1982 Marketing Data Book Issue.

Rank	Sales	Model	Rank	Sales	Model	Rank	Sales	Model
100.	11,533	RENAULT R-18	132.	3,251	PORSCHE 924	164.	781	ROVER
101.	10,881	VW VANAGON	133.	3,150	DODGE 400	165.	682	BMW 528E
102.	10,680	LEBARON (K)	134.	3,018	SAAB 900S/GLE	166.	599	VOLVO GLT 2-DR.
103.	10,368	ISUZU DIESEL	135.	3,009	DELOREAN	167.	590	MERCEDES 280 CE
104.	10,228	VOLVO GL	136.	2,963	VOLVO GLT WAGON	168.	589	LANCIA ZAGATO
105.	10,037	PINTO	137.	2,882	CUTLASS CIERA	169.	555	VW QUANTUM
106.	9,359	VOLVO DL 2-DR.	138.	2,691	CENTURY (FWD)	170.	474	PEUGEOT 604 TURBODIESEL
107.	9,248	PEUGEOT 505 TURBODIESEL	139.	2,553	AUDI COUPE	171.	444	VOLVO DL DIESEL WAGON
108.	8,523	NISSAN STANZA	140.	2,454	BMW 733I			
109.	7,998	MERCEDES 380 SL	141.	2,436	MERCEDES 380 SEL	172.	418	LANCIA BETA COUPE
110.	7,437	ISUZU GASOLINE	142.	2,274	PEUGEOT 505/504	173.	322	VOLVO GL DIESEL
111.	7,380	FIAT BRAVA	143.	2,226	SAAB 900/900 GLI	174.	297	AUDI DIESEL
112.	7,377	SAAB 900 TURBO	144.	2,169	BOBCAT	175.	277	VOLVO GT
113.	6,873	FIAT STRADA	145.	2,027	TOYOTA LAND CRUISER	176.	267	VOLVO GLE WAGON
114.	6,343	FIAT X-1/9	146.	2,019	PORSCHE 928	177.	262	SAAB 99 GL
115.	6,137	AUDI 5000 DIESEL	147.	1,937	PORSCHE 924 TURBO	178.	260	MG MIDGET
116.	5,894	NEW YORKER	148.	1,756	DASHER GASOLINE	179.	232	JAGUAR XJ-S
117.	5,628	DODGE ST. REGIS	149.	1,622	SAAB 900S/EMS	180.	187	VOLVO GLT TURBO WAGON
118.	5,585	BMW 528I	150.	1,562	AUDI 4000 S-E			
119.	5,576	AUDI 5000 TURBO	151.	1,512	TRIUMPH TR-8	181.	134	LOTUS
120.	4,919	CONTINENTAL	152.	1,432	MERCEDES 300 CD	182.	111	PEUGEOT 604 SL
121.	4,649	IMPERIAL	153.	1,409	PLYMOUTH	183.	111	PACER
122.	4,618	PEUGEOT 505/504 DIESEL	154.	1,402	MERCEDES 380 SLC	184.	110	VOLVO GL DIESEL WAGON
123.	4,463	JAGUAR XJ-6	155.	1,361	CELEBRITY			
124.	4,243	TRIUMPH TR-7	156.	1,325	PONTIAC 6000	185.	64	ALFA SPRINT VELOCE
125.	4,016	PORSCHE 911	157.	1,214	ALFA ROMEO GTV 6	186.	50	LANCIA BETA SEDAN
126.	4,013	TRIUMPH SPITFIRE	158.	1,186	MERCEDES 280E	187.	45	ALFA SEDAN AUTO.
127.	3,765	VOLVO GLE	159.	1,158	ROLLS-ROYCE	188.	33	BEETLE CONVERTIBLE
128.	3,452	MG-B	160.	1,138	BMW 633 CSI			
129.	3,449	VOLVO GLT TURBO	161.	1,126	VOLVO COUPE	189.	21	ALFA SEDAN
130.	3,448	AUDI 4000 5+5	162.	1,078	VOLVO DL DIESEL	190.	19	FIAT 128
131.	3,330	MERCEDES 300TD	163.	950	ALFA ROMEO SPIDER VELOCE	191.	18	PORSCHE 930 TURBO
						192.	11	LANCIA HPE

Source: *Automotive News*, 1982 Marketing Data Book Issue.

Who Puts Tires on Old Cars?

More than thirty tire suppliers compete in the market for replacement tires. However, the top four hold more than 40% of the business. Here is *Modern Tire Dealer*'s estimate of brand shares in the replacement tire market (for passenger cars):

Goodyear	14.0%	Dayton	2.0%
Sears	9.5%	Delta	2.0%
Firestone	9.0%	Dunlop	2.0%
Michelin	8.0%	Jetzon-Laramie	2.0%
B. F. Goodrich	5.5%	Multi-Mile	2.0%
Uniroyal	4.0%	Stratton	1.5%
General	3.5%	Bridgestone	1.0%
Kelly-Springfield	3.0%	Hercules	1.0%
Montgomery Ward	3.0%	Regul	1.0%
Atlas	2.5%	Remington	1.0%
K mart	2.5%	Star	1.0%
J. C. Penney	2.5%	Summit	1.0%
Armstrong	2.0%	Western Auto	1.0%
Cooper	2.0%	Winston	1.0%
Cordovan	2.0%	Others	7.5%

Source: *Modern Tire Dealer,* January 1982.

Tire Companies Skid Out of Akron

The year 1982 marked the end of an era for the northeastern Ohio city of Akron, when General Tire & Rubber closed down its truck-tire plant there. The company said it could not afford to replace the aging facility, General Tire's original plant (it opened in 1915). When Akron Mayor Roy Ray offered special inducements such as low-interest loans and tax abatements to continue manufacturing there, General Tire held firm, saying: "Even low-interest loans have to be repaid."

The shutdown meant that no general-purpose tires, for cars or trucks, are being produced any more in the city once widely known as the "rubber capital of the world." Some plane tires are still being made in Akron by B. F. Goodrich, and Goodyear Tire & Rubber makes auto-racing and experimental tires there. General Tire, Goodrich, Goodyear, and Firestone still maintain their corporate headquarters in Akron. But all have moved tire production elsewhere. General Tire makes tires in Bryan, Ohio; Mayfield, Kentucky; Waco, Texas; Mt. Vernon, Illinois, and Charlotte, North Carolina.

Who Puts Tires on New Cars?

	Suppliers	Market Shares
General Motors	Uniroyal	36%
	Goodyear	22%
	Firestone	18%
	General	16%
	B. F. Goodrich	8%
Ford Motor	Michelin	36%
	Firestone	24%
	Goodyear	23%
	General	8%
	Uniroyal	7%
	B. F. Goodrich	2%
Chrysler	Goodyear	70%
	Firestone	14%
	General	11%
	Michelin	5%
American Motors	Goodyear	100%
Volkswagen (*Pennsylvania*)	Michelin	60%
	Goodyear	37%
	Firestone	3%

Source: *Modern Tire Dealer*, January 1982.

America's Sweet Tooth

(We Eat Less Candy But Spend More On It)

	Total Manufacturers' Sales	Per Capita Consumption
1969	$1.87 *billion*	20.2 lbs.
1970	$1.9 *billion*	19.9 lbs.
1971	$1.97 *billion*	19.3 lbs.
1972	$1.97 *billion*	18.7 lbs.
1973	$2.14 *billion*	18.5 lbs.
1974	$2.77 *billion*	17.6 lbs.
1975	$2.83 *billion*	16.1 lbs.
1976	$2.91 *billion*	16.8 lbs.
1977	$3.68 *billion*	17.3 lbs.
1978	$3.85 *billion*	16.5 lbs.
1979	$4.28 *billion*	16.6 lbs.
1980	$4.65 *billion*	15.4 lbs.

*Includes domestically produced and imported candy minus exports, except to U.S. Armed Forces overseas.

Source: U.S. Department of Commerce, Bureau of the Census from *Candy & Snack Industry*, November 1981.

Cars in Use on U.S. Roads

1951	38,515,538	1962	60,919,579	1973	89,805,159
1952	39,769,741	1963	63,493,277	1974	92,607,551
1953	42,202,349	1964	66,051,415	1975	95,240,602
1954	44,387,113	1965	68,939,770	1976	97,818,221
1955	47,377,970	1966	71,263,738	1977	99,903,594
1956	49,803,977	1967	72,967,686	1978	102,956,713
1957	51,432,460	1968	75,358,034	1979	104,676,507
1958	52,492,509	1969	78,494,938	1980	104,563,781
1959	55,086,761	1970	80,448,463	1981	105,838,582*
1960	57,102,676	1971	83,137,324		
1961	58,854,380	1972	86,438,957		

* Nearly one for every two persons. Source: *Automotive News*, 1982 Marketing Data Book Issue.

How's Your Lotus Running?

Import Car Sales in the U.S. in 1981

Lotus	136
Ferrari	779*
Rover	781
Lancia	1,068
Rolls-Royce	1,158
Alfa Romeo	2,294
DeLorean	3,009
Jaguar	4,695
Triumph	9,768
Porsche	11,241
Saab	14,813
Peugeot	16,725
Isuzu	17,805
Renault	30,869
Fiat	32,185
Fiesta (*Ford*)	32,856
BMW	41,761
Audi	50,817
Mercedes-Benz	63,059
Volvo	64,477
Volkswagen	82,173
Mitsubishi (*Chrysler*)	110,940
Subaru	152,062
Mazda	166,088
Honda	370,705
Datsun	464,805
Toyota	576,491
Total 1981 Sales:	**2,232,560**

*Ferrari's sales for 1981 were not available. This figure is for 1980.

Source: *Automotive News*, March 15, 1982.

They Try Harder

	Their Real Owners
Hertz	**RCA**
Avis	**Norton Simon**
National	**Household International**
Budget	**Transamerica**

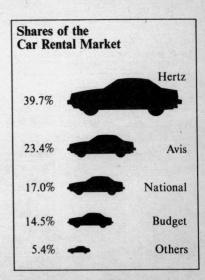

Shares of the Car Rental Market

39.7% — Hertz

23.4% — Avis

17.0% — National

14.5% — Budget

5.4% — Others

Source: *Wall Street Journal*, July 21, 1982.

Largest Seller of Used Cars

Hertz—60,000 a year

Who Fills Your Coffee Cup?

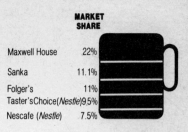

REGULAR GROUND COFFEE

MARKET SHARE

Folger's (*Procter & Gamble*)	24%
Maxwell House (*General Foods*)	20%
Hills Brothers	6%
Master Blend (*General Foods*)	5%
Sanka (*General Foods*)	3.5%

INSTANT COFFEE

MARKET SHARE

Maxwell House	22%
Sanka	11.1%
Folger's	11%
Taster's Choice (*Nestle*)	9.5%
Nescafe (*Nestle*)	7.5%

Source: John C. Maxwell, Lehman Brothers, Kuhn Loeb. Reprinted with permission from *Advertising Age*, April 12, 1982. Copyright © 1982 by Crain Communications.

The Orange Juice Market: $2.5 Billion a Year

Minute Maid (Coca-Cola)
$375 million frozen concentrate
$220 million chilled ready-to-drink

Tropicana (Beatrice Foods)
$52 million frozen concentrate
$215 million chilled ready-to-drink

Store labels
$775 million frozen concentrate
$170 million chilled ready-to-drink

Other brands (Tree-Sweet, Snow Crop, Donald Duck, etc.)
$225 million frozen concentrate
$305 million chilled ready-to-drink

Source: *Wall Street Journal*, October 8, 1982.

How to Eat Lettuce
The $640 million salad dressing business

Share of Market

Kraft*	27.6%
Wish-Bone	16.5%
Hidden Valley	15.4% (*dry*)
Good Seasons	10.9% (*dry*)
Seven Seas	10.6%

Top Flavors
1. Italian
2. French
3. Buttermilk

*Kraft has fifty flavors of salad dressings.

The Soda Pop Leaders*

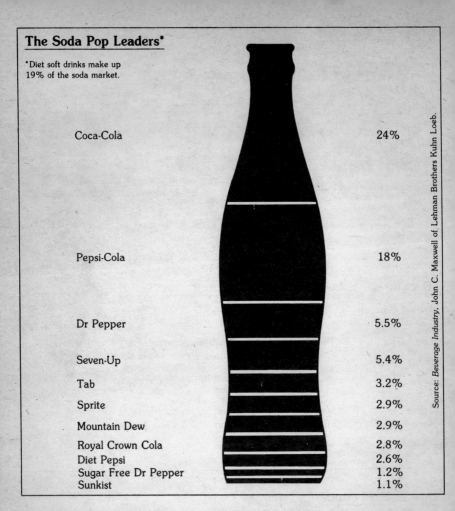

*Diet soft drinks make up 19% of the soda market.

Coca-Cola	24%
Pepsi-Cola	18%
Dr Pepper	5.5%
Seven-Up	5.4%
Tab	3.2%
Sprite	2.9%
Mountain Dew	2.9%
Royal Crown Cola	2.8%
Diet Pepsi	2.6%
Sugar Free Dr Pepper	1.2%
Sunkist	1.1%

Source: *Beverage Industry*, John C. Maxwell of Lehman Brothers Kuhn Loeb.

Popping to the Top

With annual sales of $200 million, the leading popcorn brands are Orville Redenbacher's Gourmet Popping Corn (Norton Simon) with 16% of the market; Jolly Time (American Pop Corn Co.) with 13%; and Jiffy Pop (American Home Products) with 9%. Recent entries include Micro-Pop (Austin-Kane), the first microwave popcorn that doesn't have to be frozen prior to being used; Cracker Jack Extra Fresh Popping Corn (Borden); and Hungry Jack microwave popcorn (Pillsbury).

One Big Happy Family

Mars: M&Ms, Uncle Ben's rice, Kal Kan dog food.

The Top Ten Cold Cereals

	Market Share	
	By Pounds Sold	**By Dollar Sales**
1. Corn Flakes (*Kellogg*)	6.8%	4.6%
2. Cheerios (*General Mills*)	5.6%	5.9%
3. Sugar Frosted Flakes (*Kellogg*)	5.3%	4.9%
4. Raisin Bran (*Kellogg*)	4.5%	4.0%
5. Chex (*Ralston Purina*)	4.2%	4.0%
6. Shredded Wheat (*Nabisco*)	4.2%	3.2%
7. Rice Krispies (*Kellogg*)	3.9%	4.3%
8. Raisin Bran (*General Foods*)	3.6%	3.2%
9. Grape-Nuts (*General Foods*)	3.3%	2.6%
10. Cap'n Crunch (*Quaker*)	3.1%	3.7%
	44.5%	40.4%

Source: *Advertising Age*, June 14, 1982.

It's Snickers All the Way: Top Candy Bar Sellers*

* *Before E.T.*

7.

1.

4.

8.

2.

5.

9.

3.

6.

10.

10 Biggest Fast Food Chains

		Number of Restaurants	Sales
1.	McDonald's	6,739	$7.1 billion
2.	Kentucky Fried Chicken (*Heublein*)	6,357	$2.2 billion
3.	Burger King (*Pillsbury*)	3,022	$2.1 billion
4.	Wendy's	2,229	$1.4 billion
5.	Dairy Queen	4,782	$1.1 billion
6.	Pizza Hut (*PepsiCo*)	3,995	$1.0 billion
7.	Hardee's	1,408	$910 million
8.	Denny's	1,708	$812 million
9.	Howard Johnson's (*Imperial Group*)	1,100	$630 million
10.	Jack in the Box (*Ralston Purina*)	882	$578 million

Source: *Restaurant Hospitality*, June 1982.

The Top Ten Imported Wines

		SHARE OF IMPORTED WINE MARKET
1.	RIUNITE (*Italy*)	26.4%
2.	CELLA (*Italy*)	6.5%
3.	BOLLA (*Italy*)	3.8%
4.	FOLONARI (*Italy*)	3.7%
5.	ZONIN (*Italy*)	3.5%
6.	GIACOBAZZI (*Italy*)	3.3%
7.	BLUE NUN (*Germany*)	3.1%
8.	MATEUS (*Portugal*)	3.1%
9.	YAGO SANT'GRIA (*Spain*)	2.6%
10.	LANCERS (*Portugal*)	2.1%

Source: *Impact*, March 1, 1982.

This Beer's for You: America's Favorite Beers

		1981 SALES
1.	BUDWEISER	38 *million* barrels
2.	MILLER HIGH LIFE	23 *million* barrels
3.	MILLER LITE	15 *million* barrels
4.	COORS	10.4 *million* barrels
5.	PABST	9.9 *million* barrels
6.	MICHELOB	8.3 *million* barrels
7.	SCHLITZ	6.6 *million* barrels
8.	STROH'S	5.7 *million* barrels
9.	OLD STYLE	5.2 *million* barrels
10.	OLD MILWAUKEE	5.1 *million* barrels

Source: Sanford C. Bernstein & Company, Inc.

Italian Wines Demolish the French

Import Market Shares

	1960	1965	1970	1975	1981
ITALY	35.1%	26.9%	18.4%	29.8%	59.4%
FRANCE	37.2%	39.8%	32.6%	18.6%	14.9%

Source: *Impact* © 1982.

10 Biggest Restaurants

		1981 Sales
1.	**Windows on the World** New York	$19.9 million
2.	**Tavern on the Green** New York	16.9 million
3.	**Anthony's Pier 4** Boston	12.3 million
4.	**Spanger's Fish Grotto** Berkeley, California	11.0 million
5.	**"21" Club** New York	10.0 million
6.	**Rosie O'Grady's** Orlando, Florida	9.5 million
7.	**Market Square** New York	8.5 million
8.	**Zehnder's** Frankenmuth, Michigan	8.3 million
9.	**Mai-Kai** Ft. Lauderdale, Florida	8.2 million
10.	**Frankenmuth Bavarian Inn** Frankenmuth, Michigan	7.5 million

Source: *Restaurant Hospitality*, June 1982.

One Big Happy Family

American Home Products
Preparation H, Brach chocolates
3-in-1 oil, Ecko pots and pans
Inderal high blood pressure drug
Chef-Boy-Ar-Dee canned
  spaghetti

We Drink Theirs, They Sip Ours

Wine Imported into the United States (1981): 114 *million* gallons
Wine Exported out of the United States (1981): 10.7 *million* gallons

The Best-Selling Cognacs

		MARKET SHARE
1.	HENNESSY	36%
2.	COURVOISIER	34%
3.	REMY MARTIN	11%
4.	MARTELL	9%
	OTHERS	10%

Source: *Market Watch®*, December 1981.

America's Leading Wineries*

Winery	Brands	Owner	Case Shipments
1. GALLO	Ernest & Julio Gallo, Gallo, Carlo Rossi, Boone's Farm, Thunderbird, Ripple, Paisano, Andre, Spanada, etc.	Gallo family	50.0 million
2. UNITED VINTNERS	Colony, Inglenook. Lejon, Jacare, Petri, Jacques Bonet, etc.	Heublein	20.0 million
3. ALMADEN	Almaden, Le Domaine, Charles Lefranc	National Distillers	12.7 million
4. THE WINE SPECTRUM	Taylor, Taylor California Cellars, Great Western, The Monterey Vineyard, Sterling	Coca-Cola	11.6 million
5. PAUL MASSON/THE CHRISTIAN BROTHERS	Paul Masson, Christian Brothers	Seagram**	9.4 million
6. THE WINE GROUP	Franzia, Mogen David, Tribuno	The Wine Group	6.5 million
7. CANADAIGUA WINE	Richards Wild Irish Rose, Richards, Virginia Dare, Bisceglia, J. Roget, etc.	Sands Family***	6.0 million
8. MONARCH WINE (New York)	Manischewitz, Pol D'Argent, Chateau Laurent	Star and Robinson Families	5.2 million
9. GUILD WINERIES & DISTILLERIES	Cribari, Tavola, Winemaster's, Cook's, Cresta Blanca, Roma	Farmer's Co-operative	5.0 million
10. SEBASTIANI VINEYARDS	Sebastiani	Sebastiani family	3.6 million

*Based on cases shipped in 1981.

**Seagram distributes but does not own the Christian Brothers brand, which is property of the Catholic Church.

***Approximately 25 percent of Canadiagua stock is publicly owned.

Source: L. R. Gomberg.

One Big Happy Family

General Mills: Wheaties, Izod/ Lacoste Alligator shirts, Good Earth restaurants, Parker Bros. games ("Monopoly"), Chef Saluto pizza.

The World's Biggest Drinkers

Distilled Spirits	Gallons per person		Beer	Gallons per person
1. LUXEMBOURG*	5.94		1. WEST GERMANY	38.5
2. POLAND	3.96		2. CZECHOSLOVAKIA	36.4
3. EAST GERMANY	2.97		3. EAST GERMANY	35.7
4. HUNGARY	2.97		4. AUSTRALIA	35.5
5. CANADA	2.32		5. BELGIUM	34.7
6. CZECHOSLOVAKIA	2.32		6. IRELAND	32.2
7. U.S.S.R.	2.18		7. DENMARK	32.1
8. UNITED STATES	2.03		8. LUXEMBOURG	32.0
9. WEST GERMANY	2.03		9. NEW ZEALAND	31.2
10. SPAIN	1.98		10. ENGLAND	30.9
11. FINLAND	1.84		11. AUSTRIA	26.9
12. SWEDEN	1.82		12. UNITED STATES	24.3
13. NETHERLANDS	1.79		13. CANADA	23.1
14. FRANCE	1.67		14. HUNGARY	22.8
15. NEW ZEALAND	1.65		15. NETHERLANDS	22.8
16. SURINAME	1.65		16. SWITZERLAND	18.2
17. BELGIUM	1.56		17. BULGARIA	15.2
18. ROMANIA	1.52		18. FINLAND	15.2
19. ICELAND	1.49		19. SPAIN	14.1
20. SWITZERLAND	1.35		20. VENEZUELA	13.2

Wine	Gallons per person
1. FRANCE	25.2
2. ITALY	24.6
3. ARGENTINA	19.8
4. PORTUGAL	18.5
5. SPAIN	17.1
6. LUXEMBOURG	12.7
7. SWITZERLAND	12.5
8. CHILE	11.9
9. GREECE	11.9
10. AUSTRIA	9.5
11. HUNGARY	9.2
12. ROMANIA	7.6
13. YUGOSLAVIA	7.2
14. WEST GERMANY	6.8
15. URUGUAY	6.6
16. BULGARIA	5.8
17. BELGIUM	5.4
18. AUSTRALIA	4.6
19. CZECHOSLOVAKIA	4.1
20. U.S.S.R.	3.8

*Luxembourg's actual per capita per year rate is probably much lower: many people from neighboring countries buy their booze in Luxembourg since it's cheaper there.

Source: *Impact*, January 1 and 15, 1982.

Who Sells the Most Groceries in Your Town?

A Look at the Ten Biggest Metropolitan Markets: Leading Supermarket Chains

1. NEW YORK TOTAL FOOD STORE SALES: $7.9 BILLION

	NO. OF STORES	SHARE OF MARKET
Waldbaum	64	6.6%
A&P	122	5.9%
Grand Union	69	4.2%
Shopwell	69	3.9%
Pathmark	24	2.8%

2. LOS ANGELES–LONG BEACH TOTAL FOOD STORE SALES: $7.6 BILLION

	NO. OF STORES	SHARE OF MARKET
Lucky	73	8.5%
Von's	73	7.2%
Safeway	85	6.7%
Alpha Beta	90	6.6%
Market Basket	48	4.0%
Albertson's	41	3.7%

3. CHICAGO TOTAL FOOD STORE SALES: $6.4 BILLION

	NO. OF STORES	SHARE OF MARKET
Jewel	171	24.2%
Dominicks	71	11.9%
A&P	81	6.5%
Lucky	44	5.6%

4. DETROIT TOTAL FOOD STORE SALES: $4.5 BILLION

	NO. OF STORES	SHARE OF MARKET
Bormans	84	15.7%
Kroger	51	7.8%
Chatham	46	12%
Allied	33	5.5%

5. PHILADELPHIA TOTAL FOOD STORE SALES: $4.3 BILLION

	NO. OF STORES	SHARE OF MARKET
Acme	118	17.9%
A&P	67	8.8%
Pathmark	19	5.7%
Genuardi	14	2%
Shopping Cart	15	1.7%

6. SAN FRANCISCO–OAKLAND TOTAL FOOD STORES SALES: *$3.6 BILLION*

	NO. OF STORES	SHARE OF MARKET
Safeway	107	19.7%
Lucky	63	11.9%
Cala	22	3.9%
Alpha Beta	22	3.4%
Fry's	11	2.5%
Berkeley Co-op	13	1.8%
Ralph's	7	1.4%

7. HOUSTON TOTAL FOOD STORE SALES: *$3.3 BILLION*

	NO. OF STORES	SHARE OF MARKET
Weingarten	64	14.1%
Safeway	45	11.9%
Kroger	38	9.3%
Randall's	15	6.6%
Lucky	18	5.5%

8. DISTRICT OF COLUMBIA TOTAL FOOD STORE SALES: *$3.2 BILLION*

	NO. OF STORES	SHARE OF MARKET
Safeway	133	25.3%
Giant Food	87	21.0%
Grand Union	40	8.5%
A&P	36	7.7%

9. BOSTON-LAWRENCE-HAVERHILL-LOWELL TOTAL FOOD STORE SALES: *$3.1 BILLION*

	NO. OF STORES	SHARE OF MARKET
Stop & Shop	41	9.6%
Star	37	8.6%
First National	42	7.0%
DeMoulas Market Basket	16	6.3%

10. DALLAS–FORT WORTH TOTAL FOOD STORE SALES: *$2.7 BILLION*

	NO. OF STORES	SHARE OF MARKET
Safeway	105	21.2%
Minyard	50	9.1%
Kroger	33	7.9%
Tom Thumb	41	7.5%

Where America Shops: The Top Ten Grocers

	1981 Sales	Employ
1. Safeway Stores (*Oakland*) Operates some 2,000 supermarkets in the U.S., mainly in the West, with a big division in the Washington, D.C., area.	$16.5 *billion*	157,411
2. Kroger (*Cincinnati*) Has 1,250 supermarkets in 21 states, mainly in the Midwest and South. Sales include $700 million done by 515 SupeRx drugstores.	$11.2 *billion*	127,271
3. Lucky's Stores (*Dublin, California*) Lucky's 530 food stores, operating under the names Lucky and Food Basket (in the West), Eagle (in the Southwest and Midwest), and Kash N' Karry (in Florida), do $4.6 billion of this sales volume. The rest comes from a variety of other stores—membership department (Gemco and Memco), apparel (Pic-A-Dilly), fabric (Hancock's), and automotive (Kragen, Dorman's, Checker).	$7.2 *billion*	66,000
4. American Stores (*Salt Lake City*) Result of a 1979 merger that joined Delaware's American Stores (the Acme supermarket chain) with Utah's Skaggs (Skaggs drugstores and Skaggs combination food-and-drugstores), American operates 1,140 stores in 28 states—there are 360 Acme markets in the East and 325 Alpha Beta markets in the West. In addition to the Skaggs drugstores in the West, there are 145 Rea and Derick drugstores in the East.	$7.1 *billion*	64,000
5. Great Atlantic & Pacific Tea (*Montvale, New Jersey*) Ah, the once-supreme A&P chain, down to 1,500 stores, losing money steadily. Germany's Tenglemann Group owns half the stock.	$6.5 *billion*	60,000

Suncare Market Leaders

With total annual sales of $225 million, the largest share of the suncare market belongs to Coppertone, with 40%, and Hawaiian Tropic, with 23%. Sunscreens now have one-third of the total market. Leading this segment are Sundown, with 22% and Eclipse, with 13%.

6. Winn-Dixie (*Jacksonville, Florida*) $6.4 *billion*   63,000
   Operates 1,220 nonunionized supermarkets in 12
   southern states and the southern tip of Indiana.

7. Southland (*Dallas*) $5.6 *billion*   49,600
   The 7-11 operator. Now has more than 7,000 units
   in the U.S., 40% of them franchised, 87% open 24
   hours. Also owns the Gristede's carriage trade
   groceries in New York and 265 automotive stores
   (Chief Auto Parts).

8. Jewel Companies (*Chicago*) $5.1 *billion*   37,000
   The supermarkets—345 of them operating under
   the Jewel, Buttrey, Eisner, and Star names—do
   about $3 billion of this sales volume. Also in the
   Jewel corral are the 280 Osco drugstores in the
   Midwest and the 145 Sav-On drugstores in
   California. There are also 240 White Hen
   convenience stores.

9. Grand Union (*Elmwood Park, New Jersey*) $4.1 *billion*   36,000
   Operates 860 supermarkets in 17 states in the East
   and South. Owned by France's Generale
   Occidentale.

10. Albertson's (*Boise, Idaho*) $3.4 *billion*   30,300
    Operates more than 400 supermarkets in 15 western
    and southern states. Derives nearly one-third of
    sales from 73 combination food/drugstores in
    Alabama, Florida, Louisiana and Texas.

Source: *Progressive Grocer's* MARKETING GUIDEBOOK, 1982 edition. Copyright © 1982 by Maclean
Hunter Media Inc. All rights reserved. Reprinted with permission.

Some Heavyweight Sellers

*The Marlboro cigarette brand accounts for
sales of $3.8 billion a year around the world.*

Pampers disposable diapers account for $1 billion of
Procter & Gamble's $12 billion in sales.

Top 10 Drugstore Sellers

By Units

1. Crest Toothpaste
2. Kodak Kodacolor II
3. Tylenol Tablets
4. Chapstick Lip Balm
5. Good News Disposable Razor Blades
6. Tylenol Extra Strength Capsules*
7. Rolaids
8. Similac RTF
9. Tampax
10. Q-Tips

By Dollars

1. Polaroid SX70 Film
2. Kodak Kodacolor Film C110
3. Tylenol Tablets
4. Pampers
5. Crest
6. Tylenol Extra Strength Caps
7. Dexatrim
8. Kodak Instant Film PR10
9. Oil of Olay
10. Kodak Kodacolor C135

*Prior to the 1982 temporary withdrawal from the market.

Source: Reprinted by permission from: *Drug Store News*, July 26, 1982. Copyright © Lebhar-Friedman, Inc., 425 Park Avenue, New York, NY 10022.

The 90 Million Dollar Itch

	Market Share
Preparation H (*American Home Products*)	55%
Tronolane (*Abbott Labs*)	9%
Anusol (*Warner-Lambert*)	9%
Tucks (*Warner-Lambert*)	7%
Nupercainal (*Ciba-Geigy*)	6%

Total market: $90 million a year.

Nothing to Sneeze At

$1.2 Billion Cold Remedy Market

MARKET SHARE

NYQUIL (*Richardson-Vicks*)	19%
COMTREX (*Bristol-Myers*)	13%
CONTAC (*SmithKline*)	12%
DRISTAN (*American Home Products*)	10%
CO-TYLENOL (*Johnson & Johnson*)	7%
ALKA-SELTZER PLUS (*Miles Labs*)	5%
CORICIDIN (*Schering-Plough*)	5%

Source: *Advertising Age*, May 10, 1982.

Leading Hand Lotions

	Market Share
1. Vaseline Intensive Care (*Chesebrough-Pond's*)	30%
2. Jergens (*American Brands*)	12%
3. Soft Sense (*S. C. Johnson*)	10%
4. Wondra (*Procter & Gamble*)	8%
5. Vaseline Dermatology Formula (*Chesebrough-Pond's*)	5%
6. Jergens Aloe & Lanolin	5%

P & G's Detergent Mob

	MARKET SHARE
1. TIDE (*Procter & Gamble*)	24%
2. CHEER (*Procter & Gamble*)	9%
3. WISK (*Lever Bros.*)	7%
4. FRESH START (*Colgate-Palmolive*)	5%
5. ERA (*Procter & Gamble*)	6%
6. BOLD (*Procter & Gamble*)	5%
7. DASH (*Procter & Gamble*)	3%

Source: *Advertising Age,* 100 Leaders issue.

Deodorizing America

	MARKET SHARE
1. Ivory (*Procter & Gamble*)	18%
2. Dial (*Greyhound*)	14%
3. Zest (*Procter & Gamble*)	10%
4. Safeguard (*Procter & Gamble*)	7%
5. Coast (*Procter & Gamble*)	7%
6. Dove (*Lever Bros.*)	6%
7. Irish Spring (*Colgate-Palmolive*)	5%
8. Camay (*Procter & Gamble*)	4%

Source: *Advertising Age,* 100 Leaders issue, 1982.

The Underarm Leaders

	MARKET SHARE
1. Secret (*Procter & Gamble*)	14%
2. Sure (*Procter & Gamble*)	13%
3. Arrid (*Carter-Wallace*)	12.5%
4. Right Guard (*Gillete*)	10%
5. Ban (*Bristol-Myers*)	9%
6. Mennen	7%
7. Dry Idea (*Gillette*)	6%
8. Soft 'n Dri (*Gillette*)	5%
9. Old Spice (*Shulton*)	5%

Source: *Advertising Age,* 100 Leaders issue, 1982.

The Aching Joint Market

$600 Million a Year Top Prescription Anti-Arthritic Drugs

	MANUFACTURER	MARKET SHARE
Motrin	Upjohn	25.8%
Naprosyn	Syntex	20.9%
Clinoril	Merck	16.7%
Indocin	Merck	12.6%
Nalfon	Eli Lilly	5.6%
Feldene	Pfizer	5.6%
Tolectin	Johnson & Johnson	5.0%
Meclomen	Warner Lambert	4.3%
Oraflex*	Eli Lilly	2.8%
Ridaura	SmithKline	0.7%

* Lilly withdrew this product in 1982 after it was linked to dangerous side effects.

Source: Statistics © 1982 by the New York Times Company. Reprinted by permission.

Collaring the Flea Market

Annual sales of Flea Collars are $175 million. Locked in a dogfight for the lead are Hartz Mountain, with 45% of the market and Sergeants (A. H. Robins), with 25% of the market.

Source: *Advertising Age,* January 25, 1982.

How the World Typewriter Market Shapes Up:
2.7 Million Electrics Sold in 1980

IBM	48.0%	HERMES	6.0
TRIUMPH ADLER	13.6%	OTHERS	4.4%
OLIVETTI	12.6%		
OLYMPIA	9.2%		
FACIT	6.2%		

Source: *Financial Times,*
September 17, 1981.

The 35mm King

Of the 3.4 million 35mm cameras sold in the world during 1981, 1.2 million were Canons.

Only Head of Major Company Who Was Born in Germany

W. Michael Blumenthal, chairman of Burroughs

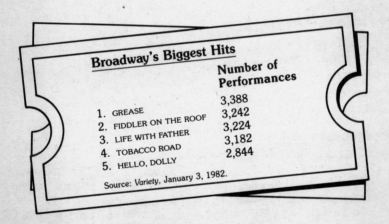

Broadway's Biggest Hits

		Number of Performances
1.	GREASE	3,388
2.	FIDDLER ON THE ROOF	3,242
3.	LIFE WITH FATHER	3,224
4.	TOBACCO ROAD	3,182
5.	HELLO, DOLLY	2,844

Source: *Variety*, January 3, 1982.

Movie Champs: The Film Rental Leaders

1.	STAR WARS (*Fox*, 1977)	$185,138,000*
2.	THE EMPIRE STRIKES BACK (*Fox*, 1980)	$134,209,000
3.	JAWS (*Universal*, 1975)	$133,435,000
4.	GREASE (*Paramount*, 1978)	$ 96,300,000
5.	RAIDERS OF THE LOST ARK (*Paramount*, 1981)	$ 90,434,000

Source: *Variety*, January 13, 1982.

*Based on film rentals collected by distributor.

Top-Selling Golf Balls

Annual Market:

215 million golf balls

$200 million in sales

1. TITLEIST (40% of the market)
2. SPALDING
3. WILSON
4. DUNLOP

Top-Selling Tennis Rackets

1. WILSON (30% market share)
2. HEAD
3. PRINCE
4. DUNLOP

The Hi-Fi Market

Whatever Happened to RCA, GE, and Zenith?

The Top Suppliers in the Stereo Business (amplifiers, receivers, speakers, tuners, and turntables)

	1981 SALES
PIONEER	$170 *million*
PANASONIC (*Matsushita*)	$170 *million*
FISHER (*Sanyo*)	$110 *million*
SONY	$80 *million*
JVC (*Japan Victor Co.*)	$80 *million*
SANSUI	$60 *million*
KENWOOD	$50 *million*
YAMAHA	$50 *million*

Source: *New York Times*, May 23, 1982. Copyright © 1982 by the New York Times Company. Reprinted by permission.

Our Biggest Trading Partners

IMPORTERS

The top ten buyers of U.S.-made goods in 1981—and the amount they bought, in dollars, were:

1. CANADA — $39.6 *billion*
2. JAPAN — $21.8 *billion*
3. MEXICO — $17.8 *billion*
4. BRITAIN — $12.4 *billion*
5. WEST GERMANY — $10.3 *billion*
6. NETHERLANDS — $8.6 *billion*
7. FRANCE — $7.3 *billion*
8. SAUDI ARABIA — $7.3 *billion*
9. BELGIUM — $5.8 *billion*
10. ITALY — $5.4 *billion*

EXPORTERS

The top ten exporters of goods to the United States in 1981—and the amount they sold us, in dollars, were:

1. CANADA — $46.4 *billion*
2. JAPAN — $37.6 *billion*
3. SAUDI ARABIA — $14.4 *billion*
4. MEXICO — $13.7 *billion*
5. BRITAIN — $12.8 *billion*
6. WEST GERMANY — $11.4 *billion*
7. NIGERIA — $9.2 *billion*
8. TAIWAN — $8 *billion*
9. FRANCE — $5.7 *billion*
10. VENEZUELA — $5.6 *billion*

Source: U.S. Department of Commerce.

So You Think Your Insurance Premium Is High?

The Tennessee Valley Authority pays $6.4 million a year to insure its five nuclear reactors against damages that might result from natural disasters such as flood or hurricane. The reactors are insured up to $900 million on a policy issued by Nuclear Mutual Ltd., of Hamilton, Bermuda.

35

The Top-Selling Cigars

The Big Ones | Market Share

Rank	Cigar	Market Share
1.	King Edward	19.7%
2.	Muriel	9.3%
3.	Dutch Masters	8.2%
4.	White Owl	7.0%
5.	Phillies	5.1%
6.	El Producto	5.0%
7.	Antonio y Cleopatra	4.7%
8.	Robert Burns	4.3%
9.	Havatampa	4.1%
10.	William Penn	3.6%

And the Little Ones

Rank	Cigar	Market Share
1.	Winchester	56.1%
2.	Dutch Treats	26.9%
3.	Omega	4.6%
4.	Between the Acts	3.2%
5.	Madison	2.2%

Source: John C. Maxwell, of Lehman Brothers Kuhn Loeb. Reprinted with permission from *Advertising Age*. June 7, 1982. Copyright (c) 1982 by Crain Communications Inc.

World's Top 20 Airlines

(By Number of Passengers Carried)

1.	AEROFLOT	100,000,000*
2.	EASTERN	35,515,000
3.	DELTA	34,800,000
4.	UNITED	29,162,345
5.	AMERICAN	24,712,562
6.	ALL NIPPON	22,421,000
7.	TWA	18,003,411
8.	REPUBLIC	16,841,000
9.	BRITISH AIRWAYS	15,272,000
10.	AIR CANADA	14,191,797
11.	LUFTHANSA	13,894,356
12.	JAPAN AIR LINES	13,880,000
13.	PAN AM	13,544,000
14.	US AIR	13,493,928
15.	IBERIA	13,234,355
16.	AIR FRANCE	11,591,907
17.	NORTHWEST	11,144,785
18.	BRANIFF	19,494,611
19.	SAUDIA	9,383,000
20.	CONTINENTAL	9,113,000

*Aeroflot, the Soviet Union's airline, is believed to have carried more than 100 million passengers—but there are no official figures available.

Source: *Airline Executive*, May 1982.

America's Favorite Ways to Fly

	Revenue Passenger Miles*	Passengers Flown			
UNITED	35.3 billion	29.2 million	AIR FLORIDA	2.4 billion	2.7 million
PAN AM	29.9 billion	13.5 million	SOUTHWEST	2.3 billion	6.8 million
AMERICAN	27.8 billion	24.7 million	TEXAS INTER-NATIONAL	2.2 billion	3.4 million
EASTERN	26.1 billion	35.5 million	PSA	2.1 billion	6.1 million
TWA	25.8 billion	18.0 million	OZARK	1.9 billion	4.3 million
DELTA	24.2 billion	34.8 million	FLYING TIGERS	1.8 billion	0.4 million
NORTHWEST	14.3 billion	11.1 million	AIR CAL	1.3 billion	3.5 million
CONTINENTAL	13.7 billion	8.4 million	ALASKA	1.0 billion	1.3 million
BRANIFF	8.9 billion	10.5 million			
WESTERN	8.5 billion	8.4 million			
REPUBLIC	7.6 billion	16.8 million			
USAIR	5.5 billion	13.5 million			
WORLD	5.4 billion	2.0 million			
FRONTIER	3.5 billion	4.9 million			
PIEDMONT	3.2 billion	7.3 million			
TRANSAMERICA	3.0 billion	0.8 million			
CAPITOL AIR	2.8 billion	1.2 million			

*The airline industry commonly uses the term "Revenue Passenger Miles" to compare airlines. It takes into account how far passengers are carried as well as how many are flown. Thus a 1,000-mile flight that carries 75 paying passengers is said to have flown 75,000 Revenue Passenger Miles. These figures are for 1981.

Source: *Airline Executive*, 1982.

Words with wings

Match the Airline with Its Slogan:

Airline	Slogan
AMERICAN	1. The Only Way to Fly
USAIR	2. You're Going to Like Us
UNITED	3. Doing What We Do Best
PAN AM	4. Fly the Friendly Skies
EASTERN	5. Nobody Serves the Public Like . . .
DELTA	6. You Should See Us Now
WESTERN	7. The World's Most Experienced Airline
TWA	8. Ready When You Are
PIEDMONT	9. Fly the U.S.A. on . . .
CONTINENTAL	10. America's Favorite Way to Fly
REPUBLIC	11. Once You've Flown with Us, You'll Wish We Flew Everywhere

ANSWERS: 1. Western 2. TWA 3. American 4. United 5. Republic 6. Continental 7. Pan Am 8. Delta 9. USAir 10. Eastern 11. Piedmont

Where Have All the Car Dealers Gone?

DATE	NUMBER OF RETAIL OUTLETS	% GAIN OR LOSS FROM PREVIOUS YEAR	DATE	NUMBER OF RETAIL OUTLETS	% GAIN OR LOSS FROM PREVIOUS YEAR
Jan. 1, 1982	21,680*	−0.41	Jan. 1, 1963	30,853	−1.53
Jan. 1, 1981	21,772	−6.87	Jan. 1, 1962	31,331	−3.54
Jan. 1, 1980	23,379	−2.79	Jan. 1, 1961	32,482	−3.49
Jan. 1, 1979	24,051	−0.40	Jan. 1, 1960	33,658	−4.05
Jan. 1, 1978	24,147	−0.50	Jan. 1, 1959	35,077	−5.68
Jan. 1, 1977	24,268	−0.76	Jan. 1, 1958	37,188	−2.09
Jan. 1, 1976	24,453	−2.11	Jan. 1, 1957	37,962	−7.40
Jan. 1, 1975	24,980	−1.46	Jan. 1, 1956	41,018	+1.60
Jan. 1, 1974	25,349	−0.36	Jan. 1, 1955	40,374	−3.66
Jan. 1, 1973	25,441	−0.70	Jan. 1, 1954	41,910	−7.26
Jan. 1, 1972	25,621	−1.93	Jan. 1, 1953	45,191	−1.79
Jan. 1, 1971	26,126	−3.49	Jan. 1, 1952	46,014	−3.22
Jan. 1, 1970	27,071	−1.51	Jan. 1, 1951	47,543	−1.54
Jan. 1, 1969	27,486	−1.07	Jan. 1, 1950	46,821	−4.78
Jan. 1, 1968	27,784	−2.24	Jan. 1, 1949	49,173	+6.60
Jan. 1, 1967	28,422	−6.14	Jan. 1, 1948	46,092	+1.12
Jan. 1, 1966	30,278	−1.35	Jan. 1, 1947	45,580	
Jan. 1, 1965	30,691	−0.44			
Jan. 1, 1964	30,827	−0.08			

Another Bad Year for Detroit

	MODEL YEAR 1982	MODEL YEAR 1981
American Motors	99,300	145,206
Chrysler (total)	658,720	764,535
Chrysler	149,628	108,129
Imperial	2,807	6,368
Plymouth	255,893	332,169
Dodge	250,392	317,869
Ford Motor (total)	1,289,983	1,487,961
Ford	888,633	1,058,044
Mercury	319,697	364,335
Lincoln	81,653	65,582
General Motors (total)	3,387,607	4,032,727
Buick	694,742	756,186
Cadillac	237,032	226,427
Chevrolet	1,234,988	1,566,391
Oldsmobile	759,000	882,505
Pontiac	461,845	610,218
Volkswagen	107,396	160,022
Total	5,543,006	6,590,451

Source: *Automotive News.*

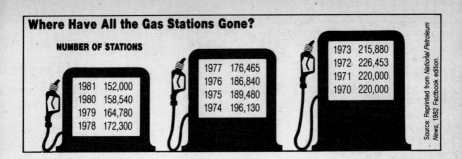

Where Have All the Gas Stations Gone?

NUMBER OF STATIONS

Year	Number
1981	152,000
1980	158,540
1979	164,780
1978	172,300
1977	176,465
1976	186,840
1975	189,480
1974	196,130
1973	215,880
1972	226,453
1971	220,000
1970	220,000

Source: Reprinted from *National Petroleum News*, 1982 Factbook edition.

Where Have All the Grocery Stores Gone?

Year	Number of Stores	Year	Number of Stores	Year	Number of Stores	Year	Number of Stores
1981	165,000	1970	208,300	1959	280,500	1948	404,700
1980	167,100	1969	219,330	1958	285,500	1947	405,500
1979	168,900	1968	226,700	1957	298,800	1946	409,000
1978	169,500	1967	226,170	1956	310,000	1945	398,400
1977	175,820	1966	227,005	1955	343,300	1944	384,400
1976	183,700	1965	227,050	1954	354,640	1943	384,100
1975	191,810	1964	228,600	1953	362,600	1942	420,400
1974	198,130	1963	231,000	1952	377,000	1941	444,850
1973	199,560	1962	234,870	1951	394,000	1940	446,350
1972	201,050	1961	248,800	1950	400,700		
1971	204,900	1960	260,050	1949	398,000		

Source: *Progressive Grocer*, April 1982. Copyright © 1982 by Maclean Hunter Media Inc. All rights reserved. Reprinted with permission.

The Filthy Five

1980
Dow Chemical
International Paper
Republic Steel
Occidental Petroleum
Standard Oil of Indiana

1981
Dow Chemical
Occidental Petroleum
Republic Steel
Standard Oil of Indiana
Weyerhaeuser

"The Filthy Five" is a designation of the Washington, D.C.-based organization, Environmental Action, which singled out companies "having a sorry environmental record and making large campaign contributions" to congressional candidates with anti-environment voting records. Environmental Action said, for example, that of the $1 million spent by the "Filthy Five" in 1979 and 1980 through their Political Action Committees (PACs), 82% went to congressmen who had "voted against the environment more than half the time."

IBM marketing representative Lloyd Johnson, former captain of the University of Southern California track team, battles General Electric's Paul Stearns for the lead in the Pyramid Relay of the 1982 Chariot Cup relays. The five-man IBM team won the event, which consists of legs of one-quarter mile, one-half mile, three-quarters mile, one-half mile, and one-quarter mile, in the time of 9:08.1. Hewlett-Packard finished three seconds behind, GE eight seconds behind. Bell Systems captured first place in the relays, dethroning two-time champion Texas Instruments.

Top 10 Corporate Track Teams

POINTS

1. Bell System	91	5. IBM	74	9. Bank of America	45
2. Texas Instruments	83	6. Hewlett-Packard	70	10. Pacific Telephone	37
3. General Electric	78	7. Montgomery Securities	69		
4. Delta Airlines	74	8. Ford Motor	67		

* Based on results of 1982 Chariot Cup relays sponsored by *Runner's World.*

III / Who's on First?

America's Biggest Weapons Makers

Total U.S. military contracts for fiscal 1981
were nearly $100 million. The top 100
defense contractors accounted for two-thirds
of the total. Number 99 on the list was
Kuwait National Petroleum Co. Ltd. ($121
million); number 100 was Transamerica,
whose United Artists film subsidiary had a
contract for $253,000. Here are the top
twenty-five:

1.	McDonnell Douglas	$4.4 *billion*	14. Exxon	$1.2 *billion*
2.	United Technologies	$3.8 *billion*	15. Tenneco	$1.2 *billion*
3.	General Dynamics	$3.4 *billion*	16. Rockwell International	$1.1 *billion*
4.	General Electric	$3.0 *billion*	17. Westinghouse Electric	$1.1 *billion*
5.	Boeing	$2.7 *billion*	18. FMC	$1.1 *billion*
6.	Lockheed	$2.7 *billion*	19. Standard Oil of California	$971 *million*
7.	Hughes Aircraft	$2.6 *billion*	20. Sperry	$928 *million*
8.	Raytheon	$1.8 *billion*	21. RCA	$877 *million*
9.	Grumman	$1.7 *billion*	22. Honeywell	$838 *million*
10.	Chrysler	$1.4 *billion*	23. IBM	$805 *million*
11.	Litton Industries	$1.4 *billion*	24. AT&T	$695 *million*
12.	Martin Marietta	$1.3 *billion*	25. Texas Instruments	$625 *million*
13.	Philbro	$1.2 *billion*		

Source: U.S. Department of Defense.

Small Town, Big Business

Despite the continuing urbanization/suburbinization of America, many industries have remained in small towns—with their headquarters offices as well as their plants.

Here is a list of fifteen well-known consumer items that are made by companies whose home offices are in cities and towns well under 100,000 population and in most cases far removed from large urban areas. Match the product with its "home town."

Products	Home Office
1. JONES SAUSAGES	A. Modesto, California
2. COOPER TIRES	B. Newton, Iowa
3. JACK DANIEL'S WHISKY	C. St. Joseph, Missouri
4. KELLOGG'S CEREALS	D. Orrville, Ohio
5. GALLO WINES	E. Janesville, Wisconsin
6. FRYE BOOTS	F. Fremont, Michigan
7. STETSON HATS	G. Golden, Colorado
8. COORS BEER	H. Fort Atkinson, Wisconsin
9. MAYTAG WASHING MACHINES	I. Marlboro, Massachussetts
10. WINNEBAGO MOTOR HOMES	J. Piffard, New York
11. SMUCKER'S JELLIES	K. Lynchburg, Tennessee
12. GERBER BABY FOODS	L. Findlay, Ohio
13. PARKER PENS	M. Battle Creek, Michigan
14. MONK'S BREAD	N. Wilton, Maine
15. BASS SHOES	O. Forest City, Iowa

Answers 1-H (Jones sausages/ Fort Atkinson). 2-L (Cooper tires/ Findlay). 3-K (Jack Daniel's whisky/Lynchburg). 4-M (Kellogg's cereals/Battle Creek). 5-A (Gallo wines/Modesto). 6-I (Frye boots/Marlboro). 7-C (Stetson hats/St. Joseph). 8-G (Coors beer/Golden). 9-B (Maytag washing machines/Newton). 10-O (Winnebago motor homes/Forest City). 11-D (Smucker's jellies/ Orrville). 12-F (Gerber baby foods/Fremont). 13-E (Parker pens/Janesville). 14-J (Monk's bread/Piffard). 15-N (Bass shoes/ Wilton).

Source: Reprinted with permission from *Advertising Age,* March 22, 1982.
Copyright 1982 by Crain Communications.

Will They Ever Run Out of Companies?

The Best-Managed Companies in the U.S., 1972–1981

For ten years *Dun's* magazine—it used to be called *Dun's Review* and now it's *Dun's Business Month* (it is owned by Dun & Bradstreet)—has been making an annual selection of the five best-managed companies in the United States. It's a selection that's widely followed in the financial community. So far, not one company has been repeated. Here is the roster of all "five best," year by year:

1972
1. DU PONT
2. EASTMAN KODAK
3. MOBIL
4. PFIZER
5. XEROX

1973
1. CITICORP
2. EXXON
3. MONSANTO
4. J. C. PENNEY
5. WEYERHAEUSER

1974
1. AT&T
2. KERR-MCGEE
3. MERCK
4. R. J. REYNOLDS INDUSTRIES
5. SOUTHERN RAILWAY

1975
1. DOW CHEMICAL
2. HEWLETT-PACKARD
3. S. S. KRESGE
4. MERRILL LYNCH
5. PROCTER & GAMBLE

1976
1. BANKAMERICA
2. BENDIX
3. HALLIBURTON
4. PHILIP MORRIS
5. RALSTON PURINA

1977
1. BEATRICE FOODS
2. DELTA AIR LINES
3. EMERSON ELECTRIC
4. GENERAL MOTORS
5. MCDONALD'S

1978
1. BOEING
2. CATERPILLAR TRACTOR
3. CONTINENTAL ILLINOIS
4. GENERAL ELECTRIC
5. SCHLUMBERGER

1979
1. AMERICAN BROADCASTING COMPANIES
2. DIGITAL EQUIPMENT
3. RAYTHEON
4. REVLON
5. UNION PACIFIC

1980
1. AMERICAN STANDARD
2. GANNETT
3. INTEL
4. PERKIN-ELMER
5. STANDARD OIL OF INDIANA

1981
1. BAKER INTERNATIONAL
2. DEERE
3. FEDERAL EXPRESS
4. GENERAL MILLS
5. TANDY

They ♡ NY

Here's a state-by-state breakdown of the headquarters locations of the Fortune 1,000—the top 1,000 manufacturing companies.

1. New York	150	16. Georgia	19	31. Arizona	5
2. Illinois	90	17. North Carolina	16	32. New Hampshire	5
3. California	79	18. Virginia	15	33. Delaware	4
4. Ohio	77	19. Florida	14	34. Louisiana	4
5. Texas	70	20. Oklahoma	11	35. Rhode Island	4
6. Pennsylvania	64	21. Oregon	10	36. Arkansas	3
7. Connecticut	56	22. Tennessee	10	37. Mississippi	2
8. Massachusetts	45	23. Maryland	9	38. Nebraska	2
9. Michigan	37	24. Colorado	8	39. Alaska	1
10. Minnesota	28	25. Washington	8	40. District of Columbia	1
11. Wisconsin	28	26. Iowa	7	41. Hawaii	1
12. North Jersey	27	27. Kansas	7	42. Idaho	1
13. Missouri	21	28. Kentucky	6	43. North Dakota	1
14. New Jersey	21	29. South Carolina	6	44. Puerto Rico	1
15. Indiana	20	30. Alabama	5	45. Utah	1

Source: *Fortune,* May 3 and June 14, 1982.

The Company with the Largest Board of Directors

Texas Commerce Bancshares, Houston (the nation's twenty-seventh largest bank and third largest in Texas after InterFirst and Republic).
Forty-four directors, including former President Gerald R. Ford, Mrs. Lyndon B. Johnson, former Congresswoman Barbara Jordan, Standard Oil of Ohio vice-chairman Thomas D. Barrow, Fluor chairman R. Robert Fluor, oilman Robert Mosbacher, Gulf Oil president Edward B. Walker III, Coca-Cola financial chief Sam Ayoub, and Dr Pepper president Charles L. Jarvie.

Corporate Conscience: The Most Remarkable Statement By a Business Leader

I cannot agree that the aged, the poor, the helpless, the unemployed, and other unfortunate Americans are not entitled to a reasonable level of public support, guns or no guns. It is my feeling that any society which cannot afford reasonable support to such people would be so poor in spirit that it should not be trusted with guns."

—The late Edward F. Gibbons, chairman, F. W. Woolworth Co., in talk to the Economic Club of Detroit, Feb. 1, 1982. Gibbons died on Oct. 26, 1982.

The 25 Largest Companies*

1.	Exxon	$107.1 *billion*
2.	Mobil	65.7 *billion*
3.	AT&T	63.3 *billion*
4.	General Motors	61.8 *billion*
5.	Texaco	51.0 *billion*
6.	Standard Oil (California)	40.2 *billion*
7.	Ford Motor	36.9 *billion*
8.	Du Pont	33.4 *billion*
9.	IBM	32.3 *billion*
10.	Gulf Oil	30.5 *billion*
11.	Standard Oil (Indiana)	30.2 *billion*
12.	Sears, Roebuck	29.2 *billion*
13.	Arco	27.0 *billion*
14.	General Electric	26.6 *billion*
15.	Phibro-Salomon	24.4 *billion*
16.	ITT	22.7 *billion*
17.	Shell Oil	20.1 *billion*
18.	Citicorp	18.3 *billion*
19.	U.S. Steel	17.9 *billion*
20.	Safeway	17.4 *billion*
21.	Occidental Petroleum	17.3 *billion*
22.	K mart	17.1 *billion*
23.	Sun	16.2 *billion*
24.	Phillips Petroleum	15.9 *billion*
25.	Tenneco	15.5 *billion*

*Ranked by sales for the 12 months ending September 30, 1982.

The Fountain of Youth in Memphis

The five largest companies in Memphis are the Federal Company, the nation's largest chicken producer; Federal Express, the fast-flying courier service; Malone & Hyde, the largest food wholesaler in the South; Holiday Inns, the world's largest innkeeper; and First Tennessee National (the largest bank in town). In 1982, Federal was headed by 41-year-old R. Lee Taylor II; Federal Express was run by founder Frederick W. Smith, who was 37 years old; Malone & Hyde's chairman was Joseph R. Hyde III, who was 39; and the president of Holiday Inns was 40-year-old Michael Rose. And First Tennessee? The boss there was a grizzled 51-year-old, Ronald A. Terry.

The 25 Most Profitable Companies*

1.	AT&T	$7.369 *billion*
2.	Exxon	4.261 *billion*
3.	IBM	3.793 *billion*
4.	Standard Oil (Ohio)	1.893 *billion*
5.	Standard (Indiana)	1.795 *billion*
6.	General Electric	1.745 *billion*
7.	Arco	1.711 *billion*
8.	Mobil	1.547 *billion*
9.	Shell	1.565 *billion*
10.	Standard Oil (California)	1.523 *billion*
11.	Texaco	1.482 *billion*
12.	Schlumberger	1.395 *billion*
13.	Eastman Kodak	1.104 *billion*
14.	Du Pont	1.021 *billion*
15.	Gulf Oil	924 *million*
16.	General Motors	915 *million*
17.	R. J. Reynolds	872 *million*
18.	Sun	834 *million*
19.	Tenneco	819 *million*
20.	Union Oil of California	815 *million*
21.	GTE	788 *million*
22.	Citicorp	774 *million*
23.	Pacific Gas & Electric	774 *million*
24.	Philip Morris	757 *million*
25.	Getty Oil	709 *million*

*Ranked by profits for the 12 months ending September 30, 1982.

Everything You Wanted to Know About the Trans-Alaska Pipeline

Route: Prudhoe Bay (North Slope) to Port of Valdez.

Terrain: Crosses three mountain ranges and more than 600 rivers. Pipeline runs elevated partway and underground partway.

Construction: 22,000 workers employed to lay pipeline.

Product: Crude oil.

Length: 798 miles.

Diameter: 48 inches.

Capacity: 1.2 million barrels per day.

Flow Rate: 7 mph, about 4.5 days beginning to end.

First output: July 28, 1977.

Owners: British Petroleum Pipelines, Inc. Sohio Pipeline Co. (now owned by BP) Exxon Pipeline Co. Mobil Alaska Pipeline Co. Phillips Petroleum Co. Union Alaska Pipeline Co. ARCO Pipeline Co. Amerada Hess Corp.

Cost: $7.9 billion.

Source: *Atlantic Richfield Company (ARCO).*

What It Would Take to Buy All Their Stock

The 25 Largest Companies
(Ranked by Market Value at the Close of 1981)

1.	AT&T	$47.8 *billion*
2.	IBM	$33.6 *billion*
3.	Exxon	$27.1 *billion*
4.	Standard Oil of Indiana	$15.3 *billion*
5.	Standard Oil of California	$14.6 *billion*
6.	Shell Oil	$13.5 *billion*
7.	General Electric	$13.0 *billion*
8.	General Motors	$11.6 *billion*
9.	Eastman Kodak	$11.5 *billion*
10.	Atlantic Richfield	$11.3 *billion*
11.	Mobil	$10.2 *billion*
12.	Standard Oil of Ohio	$10.2 *billion*
13.	DuPont	$8.7 *billion*
14.	Texaco	$8.5 *billion*
15.	Johnson & Johnson	$6.9 *billion*
16.	Procter & Gamble	$6.6 *billion*
17.	Gulf Oil	$6.5 *billion*
18.	Union Oil	$6.5 *billion*
19.	3M	$6.4 *billion*
20.	Merck	$6.2 *billion*
21.	Phillips Petroleum	$6.1 *billion*
22.	Halliburton	$6.1 *billion*
23.	Philip Morris	$6.1 *billion*
24.	American Home Products	$5.6 *billion*
25.	Sears, Roebuck	$5.6 *billion*

Source: *Forbes*, May 10, 1982.

$ 47.8 BILLION

The Top Ten Black-Owned Companies

	CHIEF EXECUTIVE	YEAR STARTED	EMPLOYEES
1. MOTOWN INDUSTRIES (Los Angeles)	Berry Gordy, Jr.	1959	215
2. WALLACE & WALLACE ENTERPRISES (St. Albans, New York)	Charles Wallace	1974	30
3. JOHNSON PUBLISHING (Chicago)	John H. Johnson	1942	1,500
4. FEDCO FOODS (Bronx, New York)	J. Bruce Llewellyn	1969	575
5. THACKER CONSTRUCTION (Decatur, Georgia)	Floyd O. Thacker	1970	442
6. SMITH PIPE & SUPPLY (Houston)	George Smith, Sr.	1976	135
7. H. J. RUSSELL CONSTRUCTION (Atlanta)	Herman J. Russell	1958	250
8. VANGUARD OIL & SERVICE (Brooklyn, New York)	Kenneth Butler	1970	51
9. JOHNSON PRODUCTS (Chicago)	George E. Johnson	1954	568
10. GRIMES OIL COMPANY (Dorchester, Massachusetts)	Calvin M. Grimes, Jr.	1940	65

. . . and the 99th and 100th companies on the roster are:

	CHIEF EXECUTIVE	YEAR STARTED	EMPLOYEES
99. MCLAUGHLIN OLDSMOBILE (Capitol Heights, Maryland)	Joseph C. McLaughlin	1977	35
100. PORTERFIELD WILSON MAZDA-HONDA (Detroit)	Barbara Wilson	1978	40

Smugglers in Their Hair

Johnson Products Co., * the ninth-largest black-owned company in the United States, has been hit hard by a massive onslaught of smuggling by Nigerians. In 1981, black marketers sold the firm's American-manufactured beauty products at prices lower than those manufactured by Johnson in Nigeria. This cost the company an estimated loss of $750,000.

"The smuggled goods are brought in on container ships, and come right through the ports," said the managing director of a local pharmaceutical company that has had its own problems with smugglers. Other entrepreneurs—Nigerians and foreigners alike—complained that a series of raids by Nigerian police on black market retailers last spring had little effect, despite the millions of dollars in contraband that was confiscated in the raids.

Johnson Products' director in Nigeria, Marilyn J. Cason, said she has been waging a price war with smugglers for over a year. When Johnson was selling its woman's hair relaxer for $20 per 16-ounce jar, the smugglers sold the same item for $18. Cason dropped the price to $16; the smugglers went down to $14. "The lowest price the smuggler could ask for hair relaxer and still make a profit was $4.60 a jar,"

TYPE OF BUSINESS	1981 SALES
Entertainment	$91.7 million
Petroleum sales	$81.9 million
Publishing, cosmetics and broadcasting	$81.1 million
Supermarkets	$80.0 million
Construction	$71.8 million
Oilfield pipe and supply sales	$57.0 million
Construction	$55.0 million
Petroleum sales	$52.0 million
Manufacturer of cosmetics and hair care products	$46.9 million
Petroleum sales	$41.5 million
Auto sales and service	$ 6.8 million
Auto sales and service	$ 6.4 million

Born Yesterday

Of the 100 largest black-owned companies in America, only 31 existed prior to 1970.

Oldest Black Company

The oldest company on the Black Enterprise 100 list is Chicago's Parker House Sausage. It was started in 1921.

Source: *Black Enterprise*, June 1982. Copyright © June 1982 The Earl G. Graves Publishing Co., Inc., 295 Madison Avenue, New York, NY 10017. All rights reserved.

Cason said. "So we dropped our price to $4.50. The smugglers then switched to Johnson's protein shampoo, and the price war began anew.

Cason said that Johnson's manufactured products cost more to produce in Nigeria than at the company's headquarters in Chicago. Among the reasons for this are higher energy costs (and frequent black-outs), the high cost of imported raw materials, and packaging costs (ten times higher than U.S. rates).

The company's president, George Johnson, opened the Ikeja factory with a $4 million investment. As required by law, 60 percent of the Nigerian operation is owned by Nigerians.

Smuggling is likely to continue as a fact of business life in Nigeria, Cason believes, but added, "We'll do better this year than we did last year." Considering the size and buying habits of Nigeria's population of 100 million, the market is big enough for all of us," she said. "We and the smugglers are here to stay."

*Chicago-based Johnson Products is the only black-owned company whose shares are publicly traded. You can buy it on the American Stock Exchange. The price of a share fell from $35 in 1972 to $3 in 1982.

By Leon Dash. Copyright © August 1982 by the Earl G. Graves Publishing Co., Inc. 295 Madison Avenue, New York, NY 10017. All rights reserved

The 25 Fastest-Growing Small Companies

(Ranked by Sales Growth, 1977 to 1981)

Inc., *a Boston-based magazine launched in 1979, covers the world of small companies the way* Fortune *covers big companies—and every year* Inc., *like* Fortune, *tracks the biggest and the fastest. It does an annual "Inc. 100" ranking of the fastest-growing, publicly owned companies. Here's how the top 25 looked in 1982:*

	Sales Growth 1977– 1981	1981 Sales	Employees	Business
1. APPLE COMPUTER (*Cupertino, California*)	43,154%	$335 *million*	2,400	Microcomputers
2. ELECTRO-BILOGY (*Fairfield, New Jersey*)	11,184%	$13 *million*	163	Medical equipment
3. FLARE (*Midland, Texas*)	7,797%	$9 *million*	100	Seismic data services
4. BIO-MEDICAL SCIENCES (*New York*)	7,159%	$80 *million*	850	Women's sportswear
5. SEISDATA SERVICES (*Houston*)	6,560%	$11 *million*	240	Seismic data services
6. VECTOR GRAPHIC (*Thousand Oaks, California*)	6,097%	$25 *million*	279	Microcomputers
7. SEAL FLEET (*Galveston, Texas*)	4,288%	$12 *million*	277	Offshore supply services
8. ASK COMPUTER SYSTEMS (*Los Altos, California*)	4,219%	$13 *million*	98	Software
9. CHEMICAL INVESTORS (*Indianapolis*)	4,183%	$38 *million*	370	Chemicals
10. RSI (*Greenville, South Carolina*)	3,996%	$63 *million*	750	Heat equipment and bottler
11. BEDFORD COMPUTER (*Bedford, New Hampshire*)	3,986%	$5 *million*	65	Graphic composition
12. MICOM SYSTEMS (*Chatsworth, California*)	3,962%	$33 *million*	503	Data communication equipment
13. TANDON (*Chatsworth, California*)	3,876%	$54 *million*	1,140	Flexible disk drives
14. AIR FLORIDA (*Miami*)	3,793%	$304 *million*	2,370	Airline
15. GULF ENERGY (*Salt Lake City*)	3,672%	$9 *million*	75	Oil, gas, coal
16. SAGE ENERGY (*San Antonio, Texas*)	3,161%	$57 *million*	350	Oil and gas

17. LEXIDATA (*Billerica, Massachusetts*)	2,760	$15 *million*	239	Display processors
18. TANDEM COMPUTERS (*Cupertino, California*)	2,610	$208 *million*	2,730	Computers
19. INTER-TEL (*Phoenix*)	2,518	$43 *million*	350	Telephone systems
20. NBI (*Boulder, Colorado*)	2,432	$58 *million*	1,079	Word processors
21. STERLING OIL (*Tulsa, Oklahoma*)	2,379	$18 *million*	270	Oil and gas
22. STERLING PIPE & SUPPLY (*Oklahoma City*)	2,228	$106 *million*	73	Oil field equipment
23. NUPEC RESOURCES (*Riverton, New York*)	2,207	$2 *million*	50	Mineral explorer
24. INTERNATIONAL GAME TECHNOLOGY (*Reno, Nevada*)	2,080	$62 *million*	525	Video games make
25. CHEMOLD (*Binghamton, New York*)	2,068	$36 *million*	416	Women's sportswea

Excerpted from the 1982 *Inc. 100,* May 1982, reprinted by permission, Inc. Publishing Company.

America's 25 Largest Privately Owned Companies

Company	Industry	Estimated 1981 Sales
1. CARGILL (*Minnetonka, Minnesota*)	Grain trader, meat packer, poultry processor (Paramount, Honeysuckle broilers), flour miller, feeds producer (Nutrena), salt miner	$28 billion
2. CONTINENTAL GRAIN (*New York*)	Grain trader, commodities broker, poultry processor (Hilbun broilers), bread baker (Arnold and Oroweat)	$15 billion
3. KOCH INDUSTRIES (*Wichita, Kansas*)	Oil marketing	$14.0 billion
4. MOCATTA METALS (*New York*)	Bullion dealer	$13.5 billion
5. BECHTEL GROUP (*San Francisco*)	Engineering & construction	$11.4 billion
6. APEX OIL (*St. Louis*)	Oil marketing	$10.0 billion
7. MARS (*McLean, Virginia*)	Candy (M&Ms, Snickers), rice (Uncle Ben's), dog food (Kal Kan)	$4.0 billion
8. HUGHES AIRCRAFT (*Culver City, California*)	Aerospace	$3.3 billion
9. GHR (*Destrehan, Louisiana*)	Oil production and refining	$3.0 billion
10. MILLIKEN (*Spartanburg, South Carolina*)	Textiles and home furnishings	$2.0 billion
11. S. C. JOHNSON (*Racine, Wisconsin*)	Johnson's wax, Pledge, Agree shampoo, Edge shaving cream, Shout, Rain Barrel, Raid	$2.0 billion
12. KENDAVIS INDUSTRIES (*Fort Worth, Texas*)	Oil driller, oilfield services	$2.0 billion
13. HILLMAN (*Pittsburgh*)	Electronics, refrigeration and transportation equipment	$1.75 billion
14. CARLSON (*Minneapolis*)	Hotels (Radisson), trading stamps (Gold Bond)	$1.6 billion
15. DUBUQUE PACKING (*Dubuque, Iowa*)	Meat packer	$1.5 billion

16. TRIBUNE (*Chicago*)	Newspapers (*Chicago Tribune, New York Daily News*)	$1.4 billion
17. ADVANCE PUBLICATIONS (*New York*)	Newhouse newspaper chain (29 dailies), magazines (*Vogue, Self, Parade, Vanity Fair*), book publishing (Random House, Knopf, Ballantine, Fawcett)	$1.4 billion
18. AMWAY (*Ada, Michigan*)	Door-to-door seller of soaps, cosmetics, Mutual Broadcasting	$1.4 billion
19. HUGHES CORP. (*Las Vegas*)	Hotel-casinos, Hughes Helicopters	$1.4 billion
20. GATES RUBBER (*Denver*)	Fan belts, hoses, couplings	$1.3 billion
21. HALLMARK CARDS (*Kansas City*)	Greeting cards	$1.3 billion
22. READER'S DIGEST (*Chappaqua, New York*)	Magazines, books	$1.2 billion
23. WARREN-KING (*Houston*)	Oil production and refining	$1.2 billion
24. HEARST (*New York*)	Newspapers (15 dailies, 28 weeklies), magazines (*Good Housekeeping, Harper's Bazaar*), radio and TV stations (10), book publishing (Arbor House, William Morrow, Avon), King Features Syndicate	$1.1 billion
25. CONGOLEUM (*Portsmouth, New Hampshire*)	Shipbuilding, vinyl flooring	$1.0 billion
HUNT OIL (*Dallas*)	Oil production	$1.0 billion

*Few of these companies offered exact sales figures to *Fortune:* some offered estimates; others refused to cooperate. A company officer at Mars said, "It will be a cold day in hell before the president of Mars talks to the press." This list combines manufacturing companies with nonindustrials such as Cargill, Continental Grain, Bechtel, and Hughes.

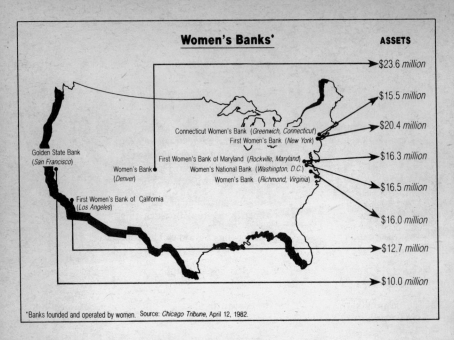

Women's Banks*

ASSETS

→ $23.6 million

→ $15.5 million

→ $20.4 million

→ $16.3 million

→ $16.5 million

→ $16.0 million

→ $12.7 million

→ $10.0 million

Golden State Bank
(*San Francisco*)

Women's Bank
(*Denver*)

First Women's Bank of California
(*Los Angeles*)

Connecticut Women's Bank (*Greenwich, Connecticut*)
First Women's Bank (*New York*)

First Women's Bank of Maryland (*Rockville, Maryland*)
Women's National Bank (*Washington, D.C.*)
Women's Bank (*Richmond, Virginia*)

*Banks founded and operated by women. Source: *Chicago Tribune*, April 12, 1982.

Top Five Black-Owned Banks

	YEAR STARTED	ASSETS	EMPLOYEES
1. Freedom National (*New York*)	1964	$127 million	84
2. Independence Bank (*Chicago*)	1964	$97 million	122
3. Seaway National (*Chicago*)	1965	$73 million	140
4. First Bank National (*Cleveland*)	1974	$69 million	65
5. Industrial Bank (*Washington, D.C.*)	1934	$61 million	80

Source: *Black Enterprise*, June 1982.

Top Ten Credit Unions

1. **U.S. Navy Credit Union** (557,000 accounts, $950 million assets)
2. **Pentagon Federal Credit Union**
3. **North Carolina State Employees**
4. **Texas Government Employees**
5. **Alaska USA Federal Credit Union** (Coast Guardsmen in Alaska, Clark Air Base in the Phillipines, employees of ten native Alaskan corporations)
6. **United Airlines Employees**
7. **Eastern Airlines Employees**
8. **Construction Equipment Credit Union**
9. **Hughes Aircraft Employees**
10. **Telephone Employees of Southern California**

Source: AP story in the San Francisco *Examiner*, based on American Banker figures.

America's 17 Largest Banks

(Ranked by Profits in 1981)

1.	Citicorp	$531 *million*
2.	Bank of America	$445 *million*
3.	Chase Manhattan	$412 *million*
4.	J. P. Morgan	$347 *million*
5.	Continental Illinois	$254 *million*
6.	Manufacturers Hanover	$252 *million*
7.	First Interstate	$236 *million*
8.	Chemical	$215 *million*
9.	Security Pacific	$206 *million*
10.	Bankers Trust	$187 *million*
11.	Interfirst	$147 *million*
12.	Texas Commerce Bancshares (*Houston*)	$137 *million*
13.	First City Bancorp of Texas (*Houston*)	$128 *million*
14.	Wells Fargo	$123 *million*
15.	Republic of Texas (*Dallas*)	$120 *million*
16.	First Chicago	$118 *million*
17.	First National Boston	$118 *million*

America's 17 Largest Banks

(Ranked by Loans)

1.	Citicorp	$77 *billion*
2.	Bank of America	$71 *billion*
3.	Chase Manhattan	$50 *billion*
4.	Manufacturers Hanover	$37 *billion*
5.	Continental Illinois	$31 *billion*
6.	J. P. Morgan	$28 *billion*
7.	Chemical	$27 *billion*
8.	Security Pacific	$21 *billion*
9.	First Interstate	$20 *billion*
10.	First Chicago	$20 *billion*
11.	Bankers Trust	$18 *billion*
12.	Wells Fargo	$16 *billion*
13.	Crocker	$14 *billion*
14.	Marine Midland	$10 *billion*
15.	Interfirst	$9 *billion*
16.	Irving	$9 *billion*
17.	Mellon	$9 *billion*

America's 17 Largest Banks

(Ranked by Assets at Close of 1981)

1.	Bank of America (*San Francisco*)	$121 *billion*
2.	Citicorp (*New York*)	$119 *billion*
3.	Chase Manhattan (*New York*)	$77 *billion*
4.	Manufacturers Hanover (*New York*)	$59 *billion*
5.	J. P. Morgan (*New York*)	$53 *billion*
6.	Continental Illinois (*Chicago*)	$46 *billion*
7.	Chemical Bank (*New York*)	$44 *billion*
8.	First Interstate (*Los Angeles*)	$36 *billion*
9.	Bankers Trust (*New York*)	$34 *billion*
10.	First Chicago (*Chicago*)	$33 *billion*
11.	Security Pacific (*Los Angeles*)	$32 *billion*
12.	Wells Fargo (*San Francisco*)	$23 *billion*
13.	Crocker National (*San Francisco*)	$22 *billion*
14.	Marine Midland (*Buffalo*)	$18 *billion*
15.	Mellon National (*Pittsburgh*)	$18 *billion*
16.	Irving Bank (*New York*)	$18 *billion*
17.	Interfirst (*Dallas*)	$17 *billion*

The Ten Largest Life Insurance Companies
(Ranked by Assets at End of 1981)

1. Prudential
   (*Newark, New Jersey*) — $62 *billion*

2. Metropolitan Life
   (*New York*) — $51 *billion*

3. Equitable Life
   (*New York*) — $36 *billion*

4. Aetna Life
   (*Hartford, Connecticut*) — $25 *billion*

5. New York Life
   (*New York*) — $21 *billion*

6. John Hancock
   (*Boston*) — $19 *billion*

7. Connecticut General
   (*Bloomfield, Connecticut*) — $15 *billion*

8. Travelers
   (*Hartford, Connecticut*) — $14 *billion*

9. Northwestern Mutual
   (*Milwaukee*) — $12 *billion*

10. Teachers Insurance & Annuity
    (*New York*) — $11 *billion*

Top Five Black-Owned Insurance Companies

	Assets	Head of Company	Year Started	Employees
1. North Carolina Mutual* (*Durham, North Carolina*)	$198 *million*	William J. Kennedy III	1899	1,345
2. Atlanta Life (*Atlanta, Georgia*)	$112 *million*	Jesse Hill, Jr.	1905	1,100
3. Golden State Mutual (*Los Angeles*)	$89 *million*	Ivan J. Houston	1925	650
4. Universal Life (*Memphis, Tennessee*)	$63 *million*	A. Maceo Walker, Sr.	1923	815
5. Supreme Life (*Chicago*)	$52 *million*	John H. Johnson	1919	310

*The 50th largest life insurance company in the United States, Sears, Roebuck's Allstate Life, has assets of $1.4 billion, or more than seven times the assets of the black leader, North Carolina Mutual.

Source: *Black Enterprise,* June 1982

Top Ten Life Insurance Companies

(Ranked by the Amount of
Life Insurance in Force at End
of 1981)*

1.	Prudential	$456 *billion*
2.	Metropolitan	$393 *billion*
3.	Equitable Life	$224 *billion*
4.	Aetna Life	$164 *billion*
5.	John Hancock	$146 *billion*
6.	New York Life	$137 *billion*
7.	Travelers	$116 *billion*
8.	Occidental Life	$124 *billion*
9.	Connecticut General	$91 *billion***
10.	Lincoln National	$73 *billion*

*Life insurance in force means the face value of all
the policies in the hands of customers. In short, if
everyone insured by Prudential died tomorrow, the
company would owe the beneficiaries $456 billion.
Now you know why insurance companies need to
have so much money.

**Connecticut General merged in 1981 with
Insurance Company of North America to form
CIGNA

The Most Anti-Union Companies

J. P. Stevens
Winn-Dixie
Texas Instruments
IBM
Delta Airlines
Texas International

World's Largest (Nongovernmental) Airline Fleet

At the end of 1981, the United Airlines fleet consisted of the following:

18 Boeing 747s (9 leased and 9 owned), each capable of carrying
between 413 and 429 passengers

46 DC-10s (31 owned, 15 leased), each capable of carrying 254
passengers

29 DC-8-61s (23 owned, 6 leased), each capable of carrying
between 190 and 238 passengers

76 B-727-222As (60 owned, 16 leased), each capable of carrying
between 132 and 158 passengers

28 B-727-222s (25 owned, 3 leased), each capable of carrying
between 132 and 158 passengers

54 B-727-100s (50 owned, 4 leased), each capable of carrying 96
passengers

49 B-737s (all owned), each capable of carrying between 118 and
125 passengers

14 DC-8-Fs (all owned), an all-cargo plane

Total: 314

America's Biggest Polluters

(Ranked by Pounds of Toxic Pollutants Spewed into the Air per Year)

1.	Monsanto	11,088,385	27.	Phillips	989,270
2.	DuPont	10,963,406	28.	B. F. Goodrich	938,100
3.	Dow	10,353,047	29.	Perstorp	731,000
4.	Amoco	6,633,400	30.	Hercor	690,800
5.	Celanese	5,451,760	31.	St. Croix	690,800
6.	Mobay	5,355,392	32.	Tenneco	634,590
7.	Hercules	4,775,400	33.	GAF	562,000
8.	Borg-Warner	4,768,300	34.	IMC	552,200
9.	Union Carbide	3,135,361	35.	Standard Oil of California	552,020
10.	FMC	2,334,000	36.	Rubicon	510,435
11.	Shell	2,330,508	37.	Commonwealth	476,924
12.	Allied Chemical	2,284,260	38.	Standard Chlorine	462,010
13.	BASF Wyandotte	1,862,930	39.	Hercofina	437,130
14.	Stauffer	1,772,208	40.	Gulf	400,010
15.	Eastman Kodak	1,708,875	41.	Diamond Shamrock	394,390
16.	Georgia-Pacific	1,694,700	42.	Corco	390,150
17.	Olin	1,624,682	43.	Goodyear	373,000
18.	American Cyanamid	1,599,290	44.	Jefferson	280,634
19.	ARCO	1,586,789	45.	ABTEC	275,400
20.	PPG	1,586,520	46.	Ashland Oil	246,075
21.	Borden	1,571,800	47.	Kalama	242,940
22.	Exxon	1,217,262	48.	Hannah Mining	225,180
23.	Sun	1,150,732	49.	Occidental Petroleum (Hooker)	224,925
24.	Vulcan Materials	1,098,330	50.	AMAX	215,460
25.	Reichold	1,055,260			
26.	U.S. Steel	1,029,434			

Unusual Corporate Directors

Robert Browne
Director of Black Economic Research Center
Saxon Industries

Douglas Fraser
President of United Auto Workers
Chrysler Corporation

Rev. Leon Sullivan
Pastor, Zion Baptist Church, Philadelphia
General Motors

George J. W. Goodman
(Author "Adam Smith")
U.S. Air

Irving Kristol
Professor of Urban Affairs, New York
University (leading conservative intellectual)
Warner-Lambert (Listerine)

John B. Connally
Former Governor of Texas, former Secretary
of Treasury
Ford Motor

Ten Worst Polluting Plants

	Company	City	Pounds Per Year*
1.	Monsanto	Decatur, Alabama	6,601,770
2.	Dow	Freeport, Texas	5,486,022
3.	Amoco	Decatur, Alabama	3,896,400
4.	Borg-Warner	Washington, West Virginia	3,892,000
5.	Celanese	Bishop, Texas	3,588,000
6.	DuPont	Laplace, Louisiana	3,220,972
7.	Hercules	Hopwell, Virginia	2,263,125
8.	Dow	Plaquemine, Louisiana	2,254,465
9.	FMC	South Charleston, West Virginia	2,184,000
10.	Shell	Deer Park, Texas	1,901,388

*Pounds per year of one or more of 33 chemicals considered by the Environmental Protection Agency as potential "hazardous air pollutants."

Source: National Clean Air Coalition; U.S. Environmental Protection Agency.

Irving Bluestone
Retired vice-president of United Auto Workers

Waterbury Rolling Mills

Gerald R. Ford
Former President of United States

AMAX, Flying Tiger, Santa Fe International, Twentieth Century-Fox

Donald F. McHenry
Former Ambassador to United Nations, now research professor at Georgetown University

Coca-Cola, SmithKline

Beverly Sills
Director of New York City Opera Company

Warner Communications

The Top 15 Companies in R&D (Research and Development)

IN TOTAL DOLLARS (millions)		IN PERCENT OF SALES	
1. GENERAL MOTORS	$2.2 billion	1. TELESCIENCES	22.1%
2. FORD MOTOR	$1.7 billion	2. KULICKE & SOFFA	18.9%
3. AT&T	$1.6 billion	3. COMPUTER CONSOLES	17.8%
4. IBM	$1.6 billion	4. AUTO-TROL TECHNOLOGY	17.2%
5. BOEING	$844 million	5. AMDAHL	17.0%
6. GENERAL ELECTRIC	$814 million	6. CRAY RESEARCH	16.0%
7. UNITED TECHNOLOGIES	$736 million	7. FLOATING POINT SYSTEMS	15.3%
8. DU PONT	$631 million	8. DYSAN	15.2%
9. EXXON	$630 million	9. INTEL	14.8%
10. EASTMAN KODAK	$615 million	10. APPLIED MATERIALS	14.4%
11. XEROX	$526 million	11. CORDIS	14.0%
12. ITT	$503 million	12. INTERGRAPH	13.1%
13. DOW CHEMICAL	$404 million	13. TERADYNE	12.7%
14. HONEYWELL	$369 million	14. GENRAD	12.6%
15. HEWLETT-PACKARD	$347 million	15. ANDERSON JACOBSON	11.8%

Rare Books: 20 Most Wanted First Editions of Modern American Fiction

1982 Value*

$500	*A Curtain of Green*, by Eudora Welty. Her first book of stories (1941).
$500	*The Moving Target*, by Ross MacDonald. First Lew Archer book (1941).
$500	*The Catcher in the Rye*, by J. D. Salinger. Cult novel of adolescence (1951).
$500	*The Moviegoer*, by Walker Percy (1961).
$400	*Lolita*, by Vladimir Nabokov (1955).
$350	*Catch-22*, by Joseph Heller (1961).
$300	*All the King's Men*, by Robert Penn Warren (1946).
$300	*Howl*, by Allen Ginsberg. Most influential post–World War II poem (1956).
$250	*Rabbit Run*, by John Updike (1960).
$200	*A Streetcar Named Desire*, by Tennessee Williams (1947).
$200	*The Naked and the Dead*, by Norman Mailer (1948).
$200	*Invisible Man*, by Ralph Ellison (1952).
$200	*Naked Lunch*, by William Burroughs (1959).
$150	*The Adventures of Augie March*, by Saul Bellow (1953).
$150	*The Assistant*, by Bernard Malamud (1957).
$125	*Death of a Salesman*, by Arthur Miller (1949).
$125	*Gravity's Rainbow*, by Thomas Pynchon (1973).
$25	*The Stories of John Cheever* (1978).

*Value for first edition in good condition (with dust jacket intact).

Source: Joseph the Provider, Santa Barbara.

IN DOLLARS PER EMPLOYEE

1.	CRAY RESEARCH	$15,060
2.	AMDAHL	$14,851
3.	AUTO-TROL TECHNOLOGY	$14,760
4.	TELESCIENCES	$11,130
5.	COMPUTER CONSOLES	$10,677
6.	APPLIED MATERIALS	$9,722
7.	INTERGRAPH	$9,393
8.	ONYX & IMI	$9,039
9.	APPLE COMPUTER	$8,532
10.	MERCK	$8,462
11.	FLOATING POINT SYSTEMS	$8,418
12.	BOEING	$8,357
13.	INTERNATIONAL FLAVORS & FRAGRANCES	$8,297
14.	CADO SYSTEMS	$8,226
15.	ELI LILLY	$8,210

Test Your Corporate I.Q.

1. Name the company that's out of place here:
Colgate-Palmolive, PepsiCo, Figgie International, AMF, Dr Pepper

2. If you had to arrange these companies in order of sales size, how would they rank?
Armco, K mart, Coca-Cola, Eastern Airlines, Hershey, Iowa Beef Processors

3. Which company is responsible for all these products?
3-in-1 oil, Brach's candies, Chef-Boy-Ar-Dee canned Ravioli, Inderal, Freezone, Dristan, Anacin, Kolynos Toothpaste

4. Where is the largest brewery in the nation and who operates it?

5. Which company has more plants in the U.S. than any other?

6. How many Japanese companies now assemble TV sets in the U.S.?

7. What company employs more teenagers than any other?

8. Which company insures more cars than any other?

Answers
1. With the exception of Dr Pepper, all these companies make sporting goods.
2. K mart, Coca-Cola, Armco, Iowa Beef, Eastern Airlines, Hershey.
3. American Home Products.
4. Golden, Colorado, near Denver, home of Coors.
5. General Electric.
6. Six: Matsushita, Sony, Sanyo, Mitsubishi, Sharp, Hitachi.
7. McDonald's.
8. State Farm.

61

The Industrial Giants:

America's Top 20 Manufacturers Over the Years

1926	SALES	1966	SALES
1. U.S. Steel	$1.5 *billion*	General Motors	$20.2 *billion*
2. Standard Oil of New Jersey	$1.3 *billion*	Ford Motor	$12.2 *billion*
3. General Motors	$1 *billion*	Standard Oil of New Jersey	$12.2 *billion*
4. Ford Motor	NA*	General Electric	$7.2 *billion*
5. Swift	$950 *million*	Chrysler	$5.6 *billion*
6. Armour	$900 *million*	Mobil	$5.2 *billion*
7. Standard Oil of Indiana	$495 *million***	Texaco	$4.4 *billion*
8. General Electric	$327 *million*	U.S. Steel	$4.3 *billion*
9. Bethlehem Steel	$304 *million*	IBM	$4.2 *billion*
10. Western Electric	$263 *million*	Gulf Oil	$3.8 *billion*
11. Gulf Oil	$254 *million*	Western Electric	$3.6 *billion*
12. Cudahy Packing	$232 *million*	Du Pont	$3.2 *billion*
13. Gcodyear	$230 *million*	Swift	$3 *billion*
14. U.S. Rubber	$216 *million*	Shell	$2.8 *billion*
15. Anaconda Copper	$213 *million*	Standard Oil of Indiana	$2.7 *billion*
16. Hudson Motors	$201 *million*	Standard Oil of California	$2.7 *billion*
17. Sinclair Consolidated Oil	$192 *million*	Bethlehem Steel	$2.7 *billion*
18. Procter & Gamble	$181 *million*	International Harvester	$2.6 *billion*
19. American Radiator & Standard Sanitary	$182 *million***	Westinghouse	$2.6 *billion*
20. Westinghouse	$166 *million*	RCA	$2.5 *billion*

*Ford Motor was privately held in 1926 and did not release exact sales figures.

**Figures for 1929.

Manufacturing

The 20 Largest Corporations Outside the U.S.

(Not a Japanese company among them)

	Country	1981 Sales
1. Royal/Dutch Shell	Britain/Netherlands	$78 *billion*
2. British Petroleum	Britain	$49 *billion*
3. Kuwait Petroleum	Kuwait	$29 *billion*
4. ENI	Italy	$27 *billion*
5. Unilever	Britain/Netherlands	$23 *billion*
6. VEBA	Germany	$22 *billion*
7. Cie Francaise des Petroles	France	$22 *billion*
8. Petroleos de Venezuela	Venezuela	$20 *billion*
9. Fiat	Italy	$18 *billion*
10. Elf Aquitaine	France	$18 *billion*

1982	SALES
1. Exxon	$108 *billion*
2. Mobil	$64.5 *billion*
3. General Motors	$62.7 *billion*
4. Texaco	$57.6 *billion*
5. Standard Oil of California	$44.2 *billion*
6. Ford	$38.2 *billion*
7. Standard Oil of Indiana	$30 *billion*
8. IBM	$29.1 *billion*
9. Gulf Oil	$28.2 *billion*
10. Atlantic Richfield	$27.8 *billion*
11. General Electric	$27.2 *billion*
12. Du Pont	$22.8 *billion*
13. Shell	$21.6 *billion*
14. IT&T	$17.3 *billion*
15. Phillips Petroleum	$16 *billion*
16. Tenneco	$15.5 *billion*
17. Sun	$15 *billion*
18. Occidental Petroleum	$14.7 *billion*
19. U.S. Steel	$14 *billion*
20. United Technologies	$13.7 *billion*

Source: *Business Week*, September 30, 1967; *Fortune*, May 3, 1982.

11. B.A.T Industries	Britain	$18 *billion*
12. Pemex	Mexico	$18 *billion*
13. Petrobas	Brazil	$17 *billion*
14. Philips	Netherlands	$17 *billion*
15. Volkswagen	Germany	$17 *billion*
16. Daimler-Benz	Germany	$16 *billion*
17. Nestle	Switzerland	$16 *billion*
18. Renault	France	$15 *billion*
19. Hoechst	Germany	$15 *billion*
20. Bayer	Germany	$15 *billion*

The 22 Largest Companies Where the Founder Is Still Around

The genius of American business magazines is to keep coming up with new lists. In 1982, Venture, *a magazine for people who venture forth to start new businesses, inaugurated the "Venture 100." This is a roster of companies (ranked by sales size) where the founder or founders remain active in the management of the business.* Venture *calls it "America's 100 largest entrepreneurial firms." Here are the top 22:*

Company	Entrepreneur(s) Date founded	1981 sales	Value of founder's holdings	Type of business
1. Coastal Corp (*Houston*)	Oscar S. Wyatt, Jr. 1955	$5.9 *billion*	$40.8 *million*	Oil and gas exploration
2. Control Data (*Minneapolis*)	William C. Norris 1957	$4.2 *billion*	$15.9 *million*	Computer hardware and software
3. Hewlett-Packard (*Palo Alto, California*)	William R. Hewlett David Packard 1939	$3.5 *billion*	Hewlett $774 *million* Packard $1 *billion*	Electronics manufacturer
4. Albertson's (*Boise, Idaho*)	Joseph A. Albertson 1939	$3.4 *billion*	$95 *million*	Supermarket operator
5. Digital Equipment (*Maynard, Massachussetts*)	Kenneth H. Olsen 1957	$3.2 *billion*	$205 *million*	Digital computers and components
6. Teledyne (*Los Angeles*)	Henry E. Singleton 1961	$3.2 *billion*	$204 *million*	Aviation, electronics, metals, insurance
7. Supermarkets General (*Woodbridge, New Jersey*)	Herbert Brody Alexander Aidekman 1958	$2.9 *billion*	Brody $10.1 *million* Aidekman $9.1 *million*	Drug and food stores (Path mark)
8. ARA Services (*Philadelphia*)	William S. Fishman 1959	$2.9 *billion*	$2.5 *million*	Food services
9. Alco Standard (*Valley Forge, Pennsylvania*)	Tinkham Veale II 1965	$2.5 *billion*	$19 *million*	Manufacturing and distribution
10. Rapid-American (*New York*)	Meshulam Riklis 1957	$2.5 *billion*	$81.8 *million*	Apparel, alcoholic beverages (Schenley), stores (Lerner Shops)

11. Wal-Mart Stores (*Bentonville, Arkansas*)	Samuel M. Walton 1962	$2.4 *billion*	$635 *million*	Regional discount department store
12. Hospital Corp. of America (*Nashville, Tennessee*)	Thomas F. Frist Thomas F. Frist, Jr. 1968	$2.4 *billion*	$41.9 *million*	Hospital management
13. Mapco (*Tulsa, Oklahoma*)	Robert E. Thomas 1960	$2.1 *billion*	$19 *million*	Exploration and production of oil and minerals
14. Stop & Shop (*Quincy, Massachussetts*)	Sidney R. Rabb Norman Rabb 1914	$2.0 *billion*	S. Rabb $7.4 *million* N. Rabb $3.9 *million*	Supermarket operators
15. Jim Walter (*Tampa, Florida*)	James W. Walter 1946	$2.0 *billion*	$7.7 *million*	Building materials, construction
16. Marriott (*Washington, D.C.*)	J. Willard Marriott, Sr. 1927	$2.0 *billion*	$34 *million*	Lodging, food, entertainment
17. Sigmor (*San Antonio, Texas*)	Thomas E. Turner 1952	$1.8 *billion*	$13.2 *million*	Independent gasoline retailer
18. Humana (*Louisville, Kentucky*)	David A. Jones Wendell Cherry 1961	$1.7 *billion*	Jones $48.9 *million* Cherry $20.4 *million*	Owner and operator of hospitals
19. Reliance Group (*New York*)	Saul P. Steinberg 1965	$1.6 *billion*	$243 *million*	Insurance, real estate, management services
20. Carlson Companies (*Minneapolis*)	Curtis L. Carlson 1938	$1.6 *billion*	N.A.	Diversified consumer products, hotels, restaurants
21. Continental Telephone (*Atlanta*)	Charles Wohlstetter 1960	$1.6 *billion*	$9.2 *million*	Telephone service and equipment
22. Polaroid (*Cambridge, Massachussetts*)	Edwin H. Land, Jr. 1937	$1.4 *billion*	$78.4 *million*	Instant cameras and film

Source: Reprinted from *VENTURE, The Magazine for Entrepreneurs*, May, 1982, by special permission.
© 1982 Venture Magazine, Inc., 35 West 45th Street, New York, NY 10036.

Who Owes the Least

DEBT

1.	Maytag	$0	39.	E-Systems	$17 *million*
2.	Adolph Coors	$0	40.	Harvey Hubbell	$17 *million*
3.	MCA	$0	41.	Commercial Metals	$18 *million*
4.	Armsted Industries	$0	42.	Genuine Parts	$18 *million*
5.	Tecumseh Products	$0	43.	Diebold	$19 *million*
6.	Dun & Bradstreet	$0	44.	Pabst Brewing	$20 *million*
7.	Weis Markets	$0	45.	Rubbermaid	$20 *million*
8.	Longs Drug Stores	$0	46.	Turner Construction	$20 *million*
9.	Petrie Stores	$0	47.	Cone Mills	$20 *million*
10.	Cannon Mills	$0	48.	Parsons	$21 *million*
11.	Stone & Webster	$1 *million*	49.	Lukens Steel	$21 *million*
12.	Homestake	$1 *million*	50.	Lubrizol	$22 *million*
13.	Northwestern Steel & Wire	$1 *million*	51.	Rorer Group	$22 *million*
14.	Stewart-Warner	$2 *million*	52.	Mitel	$22 *million*
15.	Pittway	$3 *million*	53.	A. C. Nielsen	$22 *million*
16.	SFN	$3 *million*	54.	Northrop	$23 *million*
17.	Amalgamated Sugar	$5 *million*	55.	Florida East Coast Railway	$23 *million*
18.	Carpenter Technology	$5 *million*	56.	Parker Pen	$24 *million*
19.	Communications Satellite	$5 *million*	57.	Masonite	$24 *million*
20.	Thiokol	$6 *million*	58.	R. R. Donnelley & Sons	$24 *million*
21.	General American Oil Company of Texas	$7 *million*	59.	Sanders Associates	$26 *million*
			60.	Consolidated Papers	$26 *million*
22.	Wm. Wrigley, Jr.	$8 *million*	61.	Tesoro Petroleum	$27 *million*
23.	Ogilvy & Mather International	$8 *million*	62.	A. H. Robbins	$28 *million*
24.	Chemed	$9 *million*	63.	Interpublic Group	$31 *million*
25.	De Luxe Check Printers	$9 *million*	64.	Foxboro	$33 *million*
26.	Jack Eckerd	$10 *million*	65.	Medtronic	$34 *million*
27.	Briggs & Stratton	$11 *million*	66.	Zurn Industries	$34 *million*
28.	International Flavors & Fragrances	$11 *million*	67.	Electronic Data Systems	$34 *million*
			68.	Enterra	$34 *million*
29.	Rollins	$13 *million*	69.	Cessna Aircraft	$35 *million*
30.	National Service Industries	$14 *million*	70.	Advanced Micro Devices	$35 *million*
31.	Church's Fried Chicken	$14 *million*	71.	American District Telegraph	$35 *million*
32.	Dow Jones	$14 *million*			
33.	Perini	$14 *million*	72.	Federal	$35 *million*
34.	Roadway Express	$14 *million*	73.	Dataproducts	$35 *million*
35.	Nalco Chemical	$15 *million*	74.	Cleveland-Cliffs Iron	$36 *million*
36.	W. W. Grainger	$15 *million*	75.	Amdahl	$36 *million*
37.	American Home Products	$16 *million*	76.	Loral	$37 *million*
38.	Illinois Tool Works	$16 *million*	77.	Curtiss-Wright	$37 *million*

Source: Based on Standard & Poor's Compustat Services, Inc. report of 875 of the country's largest nonfinancial corporations, ranked by assets; *Business Week*, March 1, 1982.

Who Owes the Most

DEBT

1. AT&T	$47,294,000,005	38. Florida Power & Light	$2,503,000,000
2. General Telephone & Electronics	$9,019,000,000	39. International Harvester	$2,463,000,000
		40. U.S. Steel	$2,427,000,000
3. Sears, Roebuck	$9,011,000,000	41. Gulf & Western Industries	$2,408,000,000
4. Exxon	$8,582,000,000	42. CSX	$2,310,000,000
5. Du Pont	$7,561,000,000	43. General Electric	$2,309,000,000
6. Tenneco	$6,418,000,000	44. Union Carbide	$2,307,000,000
7. Mobil	$6,314,000,000	45. General Public Utilities	$2,302,000,000
8. Standard Oil of Ohio	$6,288,000,000	46. Ohio Edison	$2,275,000,000
9. Southern	$5,639,000,000	47. Pennsylvania Power & Light	$2,191,000,000
10. Commonwealth Edison	$5,594,000,000	48. K mart	$2,095,000,000
11. American Electric Power	$5,536,000,000	49. Northeast Utilities	$2,044,000,000
12. Dow Chemical	$5,146,000,000	50. Houston Industries	$2,022,000,000
13. Atlantic Richfield	$5,110,000,000	51. Standard Oil of California	$2,001,000,000
14. ITT	$4,852,000,000	52. Cities Services	$1,969,000,000
15. Pacific Gas & Electric	$4,835,000,000	53. Carolina Power & Light	$1,965,000,000
16. Shell Oil	$4,821,000,000	54. Long Island Lighting	$1,965,000,000
17. Ford Motor	$4,383,000,000	55. United Telecommunications	$1,963,000,000
18. Middle South Utilities	$4,257,000,000	56. City Investing	$1,945,000,000
19. Standard Oil of Indiana	$3,830,000,000	57. Pacific Power & Light	$1,881,000,000
20. General Motors	$3,734,000,000	58. Georgia-Pacific	$1,834,000,000
21. Southern California Edison	$3,675,000,000	59. Tiger International	$1,810,000,000
22. IBM	$3,588,000,000	60. Amerada Hess	$1,782,000,000
23. Philip Morris	$3,371,000,000	61. Gelco	$1,781,000,000
24. Virginia Electric & Power	$3,349,000,000	62. Union Electric	$1,780,000,000
25. Avco	$3,312,000,000	63. Phibro	$1,736,000,000
26. Texaco	$3,195,000,000	64. Niagra Mohawk Power	$1,705,000,000
27. Consumers Power	$3,062,000,000	65. American Airlines	$1,643,000,000
28. RCA	$2,978,000,000	66. Central & South West	$1,642,000,000
29. Detroit Edison	$2,977,000,000	67. Weyerhaeuser	$1,641,000,000
30. Philadelphia Electic	$2,836,000,000	68. El Paso	$1,641,000,000
31. Texas Utilities	$2,802,000,000	69. Southern Pacific	$1,633,000,000
32. Chrysler	$2,800,000,000	70. Caterpillar Tractor	$1,628,000,000
33. Gulf Oil	$2,769,000,000	71. F. W. Woolworth	$1,623,000,000
34. Sun	$2,714,000,000	72. Union Pacific	$1,620,000,000
35. Consolidated Edison Co. of New York	$2,692,000,000	73. Eastern Airlines	$1,606,000,000
		74. Columbia Gas System	$1,597,000,000
36. Duke Power	$2,638,000,000	75. Hospital Corp. of America	$1,572,000,000
37. Public Service Electric & Gas	$2,506,000,000	76. W. R. Grace	$1,569,000,000

Companies Love to Change Their Names—and the Old Names Were Usually Better

Old Name	New Name
ADDRESSOGRAPH-MULTIGRAPH	AM INTERNATIONAL
ALL AMERICAN NUT COMPANY	ADAMS FOODS (*California*)
AMERICAN BRAKE SHOE	ABEX
AMERICAN MACHINE & FOUNDRY	AMF
AMERICAN TOBACCO	AMERICAN BRANDS
ARKANSAS LOUISIANA GAS	ARKLA
A-T-O	FIGGIE INTERNATIONAL
BARNABY'S FAMILY INNS	BALLY'S TOM FOOLERY
BLISS & LAUGHLIN INDUSTRIES	AXIA
CALIFORNIA PERFUME	AVON PRODUCTS
CENTRAL LOUISIANA ENERGY	CELERON
CHESSIE SYSTEM and SEABOARD COAST LINE	CSX
FIRST INTERNATIONAL BANCSHARES	INTERFIRST
COMPUTING-TABULATING-RECORDING	IBM
COPELAND	PILLSBURY
CORN PRODUCTS REFINING	CPC INTERNATIONAL
DUTCH BOY	ATRA GROUP
GENERAL SHOE	GENESCO
GREEN SHOE	STRIDE RITE
INSURANCE CO. OF NORTH AMERICA and CONNECTICUT GENERAL	CIGNA
KING'S DEPARTMENT STORES	KDT INDUSTRIES
LIBERTY NATIONAL INSURANCE	TORCHMARK
MID-WEST DRIVE-IN	GENERAL CINEMA
MINNESOTA GAS	DIVERSIFIED ENERGIES
MISSOURI BEEF PACKERS	MBPXL
MOTOR TRANSIT	GREYHOUND
NATIONAL CASH REGISTER	NCR
NATIONAL DETROIT	NBD BANCORP
NE GAS & ELECTRIC	COMMONWEALTH ENERGY SYSTEM
RAYBESTOS-MANHATTAN	RAYMARK
R. L. BURNS	PYRO ENERGY
SAFEGUARD INDUSTRIES	SAFEGUARD SCIENTIFICS
SOUTHERN NATURAL RESOURCES	SONAT
STANDARD OIL COMPANY OF NEW JERSEY	EXXON
SWIFT & COMPANY	ESMARK
TRANSCO COMPANIES	TRANSCO ENERGY
U.S. FIDELITY & GUARANTY	USF&G
U.S. RUBBER	UNIROYAL
WALLACE BUSINESS FORMS	WALLACE COMPUTER SERVICES
WESTERN BANCORP	FIRST INTERSTATE

IV/Corporate Heroes

████████████████████████████████████

Biggest Corporate Egos

Harry Gray, chairman, president, and chief executive officer of United Technologies.
He likes to sign ads and run his picture on the front cover of the annual report (he may look better than a Pratt & Whitney jet engine).

Marvin Davis, sole owner of Twentieth Century-Fox Film.
He bought all the shares and turned it into a privately owned company. "I've never gone public," he said. "I'm a free man without any stockholders, and that's the way I love it."

David Mahoney, chairman and chief executive officer of Norton Simon Inc.
Mahoney tried to get Walter Cronkite to pitch for Avis Rent-a-Car, one of Norton Simon's many companies. When that failed, he stepped into the commercials himself.

Rand V. Araskog, chairman, president, and chief executive officer of IT&T.
One-man rule is a tradition at this conglomerate, big as it is. Araskog bought a Manhattan cooperative apartment to be near his office—and he got the company to pick up the annual carrying costs: $173,000. Araskog is paid more than $1 million a year, but he saves the company money by not having a president.

Armand Hammer, chairman and chief executive officer of Occidental Petroleum.
His annual phone bill probably exceeds the salaries of most Americans. Occidental holds its annual meeting every year on Dr. Hammer's birthday (he was 82 years old in 1982). He's the only man in the world who seems to have entree in both Moscow and Peking.

Lee A. Iacocca, chairman and chief executive officer of Chrysler.
He made such a name for himself in television commericals that reports circulated that he was going to run for President of the United States, probably the only entity with a bigger deficit than Chrysler.

The Black Directors

Fifteen years ago no blacks sat on the board of a major American corporation, save for Asa T. Spaulding, retired head of the North Carolina Mutual Life Insurance Co., who was named to the W. T. Grant board in 1964 (Grant is now defunct). Today, 67 blacks sit on the boards of directors of 136 major U.S. corporations. The roster:

AETNA LIFE
Arthur Ashe, Jr.

ALCOA
Franklin A. Thomas

ALLIED CORPORATION
Jewel Plummer Cobb

ALLIED STORES
Franklin A. Thomas

AMAX
William T. Coleman, Jr.

AMERICAN AIRLINES
Christopher F. Edley

AMERICAN BROADCASTING COMPANIES
Mamie Phipps Clark

AMERICAN CAN
William T. Coleman, Jr.

AMERICAN EXPRESS
Vernon E. Jordan, Jr.

AT&T
Jerome H. Holland

AMERITRUST
Norlen M. Ellison
Doris A. Evans, M.D.

AMSTAR
Barbara Scott Preiskel

ANHEUSER-BUSCH
Sybil C. Mobley
Wayman F. Smith III

AVON PRODUCTS
Ernesta G. Procope

BANK OF AMERICA
Andrew F. Brimmer

BANKERS TRUST
Vernon E. Jordan, Jr.

BEATRICE FOODS
Walter J. Leonard

BENDIX
Jewel S. Lafontant

BORDEN
Franklin H. Williams

BURROUGHS
Wade H. McCree

CAMPBELL SOUP
Claudine B. Malone

CELANESE
Vernon E. Jordan, Jr.

CHASE MANHATTAN
William T. Coleman, Jr.

CHEMICAL BANK
Franklin H. Williams

CHRYSLER
Jerome H. Holland

CHUBB
Ernesta G. Procope

CIGNA
William T. Coleman, Jr.
Frank F. Jones

CITICORP
Franklin A. Thomas

COCA-COLA
Donald F. McHenry

CBS
Franklin A. Thomas

COLUMBIA GAS
Ernesta G. Procope

COMMONWEALTH EDISON
George E. Johnson

CONSOLIDATED EDISON
Franklin H. Williams

CONTINENTAL CORP.
Jerome H. Holland

CONTINENTAL ILLINOIS
Jewel S. Lafontant

CONTROL DATA
Lois Dickson Rice

CPC INTERNATIONAL
Jewel Plummer Cobb

CUMMINS ENGINE
Franklin A. Thomas

DART & KRAFT
Lloyd C. Elam

DELTA AIRLINES
Jesse Hill, Jr.

DETROIT EDISON
David B. Harper

DOW JONES
Vernon E. Jordan, Jr.

DU PONT
Andrew F. Brimmer

EASTERN AIRLINES
Willie C. Robinson

EASTMAN KODAK
Charles T. Duncan

70

ENTEX INC.
John B. Coleman

EQUITABLE LIFE INSURANCE
Jewel S. Lafontant
Clifton R. Wharton, Jr.

EXXON
Randolph W. Bromery

FEDERATED DEPARTMENT STORES
Jerome H. Holland

FIRST INTERSTATE
Ivan J. Houston

FIRST PENNSYLVANIA BANKING & TRUST
Henry G. Parks, Jr.

FOOTE, CONE & BELDING
Jewel S. Lafontant

FORD MOTOR
Clifton R. Wharton, Jr.

GANNETT
Andrew F. Brimmer

GENERAL FOODS
Jerome H. Holland

GENERAL MILLS
Gwendolyn A. Newkirk

GENERAL MOTORS
Leon H. Sullivan

GERBER PRODUCTS
Charles F. Whitten

GIRARD TRUST
Leon H. Sullivan

GOODYEAR TIRE & RUBBER
W. Howard Fort

W. R. GRACE
Henry G. Parks, Jr.
Harold A. Stevens

GREYHOUND
John H. Johnson

GRUMMAN
C. Clyde Ferguson, Jr.

JOHN HANCOCK MUTUAL LIFE
Mary Ella Robertson

HARPER & ROW
Kenneth B. Clark

HARTE HANKS COMMUNICATIONS
Jewel S. Lafontant

ILLINOIS BELL
John Hope Franklin
Barbara Proctor

IBM
William T. Coleman, Jr.
Patricia Roberts Harris

INTERNATIONAL HARVESTER
Andrew F. Brimmer

INTERNATIONAL PAPER
Donald F. McHenry

JEWEL COMPANIES
Barbara Scott Preiskel

JOHNSON & JOHNSON
Ann Dibble Cook

K MART
David B. Harper

KAISER ALUMINUM & CHEMICAL
Ivan J. Houston

KELLOGG
Delores D. Wharton

KNIGHT-RIDDER
Jesse Hill, Jr.

LEVI STRAUSS
Barbara Scott Preiskel

LOCKHEED AIRCRAFT
Leslie N. Shaw

R. H. MACY
Barbara Scott Preiskel

MANUFACTURERS HANOVER
Jerome H. Holland

MEAD CORP.
Barbara Jordan

MERCK
Lloyd C. Elam

METROMEDIA
Ivan J. Houston

METROPOLITAN LIFE INSURANCE
George E. Johnson
Robert C. Weaver

MID-SOUTH UTILITIES
Walter Washington

MISSISSIPPI POWER & LIGHT
Walter Washington

MOBIL
Jewel S. Lafontant
William J. Kennedy

MONSANTO
Margaret Bush Wilson

MORSE SHOE
Jesse Hill, Jr.

MUTUAL OF NEW YORK
C. Clyde Ferguson, Jr.

NATIONAL BANK OF NORTH
AMERICA
Clarence C. Finley

NATOMAS
Daniel A. Collins

NBD
Wade H. McCree

NEW ORLEANS PUBLIC SERVICE
Herman Smith

NEW YORK LIFE INSURANCE
Franklin A. Thomas
Margaret B. Young

NORTON SIMON
Ann Dibble Cook
Luther H. Foster

OHIO EDISON
W. A. Derrick

PAN AMERICAN WORLD AIRWAYS
William T. Coleman, Jr.
Patricia Roberts Harris

J. C. PENNEY
Vernon E. Jordan, Jr.

PENN MUTUAL
Claudine B. Malone

PEPSICO
William T. Coleman, Jr.

PFIZER
William J. Kennedy II

PHILIP MORRIS
Margaret B. Young

PHILLIPS PETROLEUM
Delores D. Wharton

POLAROID
Frank F. Jones

PROCTER & GAMBLE
Charles T. Duncan

QUAKER OATS
William J. Kennedy III

RCA
I. Owen Funderburgh

R. J. REYNOLDS INDUSTRIES
Vernon E. Jordan, Jr.

ROHM & HAAS
Ulric S. Haynes, Jr.

SAXON INDUSTRIES
Robert S. Browne

SCOTT PAPER
Patricia Roberts Harris
Claudine B. Malone

G. D. SEARLE
Daryl F. Grisham

SEARS, ROEBUCK
Luther H. Foster
Sybil C. Mobley

SEVEN-UP
Thomas B. Shropshire

SIGNAL COMPANIES
Henry G. Parks, Jr.

SINGER
Randolph W. Bromery

SMITHKLINE
Donald F. McHenry

SPERRY & HUTCHINSON
Jesse Hill, Jr.

SUPERMARKETS GENERAL
Claudine B. Malone

TEXAS COMMERCE BANCSHARES
Barbara Jordan

TEXTRON
Barbara Scott Preiskel

TIME INC.
Clifton R. Wharton, Jr.

TIMES-MIRROR
Alfred E. Osborne, Jr.

TRANS WORLD AIRLINES
Jewel S. Lafontant
Emmett J. Rice

TRAVELERS
Jewel Plummer Cobb

UNION CARBIDE
Jerome H. Holland

UNITED AIRLINES
Andrew F. Brimmer

WARNER-LAMBERT
Henry G. Parks, Jr.

WELLS FARGO BANK
Wilson Riles

WENDY'S INTERNATIONAL
Azie Taylor Morton

WESTINGHOUSE ELECTRIC
Vernon E. Jordan, Jr.

F. W. WOOLWORTH
Jarobin Gilbert, Jr.

XEROX
Vernon E. Jordan, Jr.

ZENITH RADIO
John H. Johnson

ZURN INDUSTRIES
Jerome H. Holland

The Corporate Chairman Who's Quickest at Figuring Out Rubik's Cube

Robert Kirby, chairman of Westinghouse. Time: 75 seconds.

For Real?

Which of the following brands are named for real people?

1. Mrs. Smith	4. Mrs. Paul	7. Mama Celeste	10. Philip Morris
2. Sara Lee	5. Smith Brothers	8. Dr Pepper	
3. Jim Beam	6. Betty Crocker	9. Jack Daniel	

Answers to BizQuiz

1. Real. Amanda Smith began by baking pies in her kitchen and selling them to neighbors. Her son began marketing them as Mrs. Smith's frozen pies, leading to Mrs. Smith frozen foods, a division of Kellogg's Inc. **2. Real.** Sara Lee is the daughter of Charles Lubin, the founder of Kitchens of Sara Lee. **3. Real.** The original Beam of distillery fame was named Jacob. James came along at the fourth generation. **4. Not real.** There is only a Mr. Paul. The company's originator was named Piszek, and his first partner was Paul, whose moniker the two used to label their frozen fish products. **5. Real.** "Trade" and "Mark" were William and Andrew Smith, sons of James Smith, the originator of the cough candies. **6. Not real.** In 1921, Washburn Crosby Co., the predecessor of General Mills, created the Betty Crocker name to use on replies to homemakers' requests for recipes. Crocker was the surname of a recently retired company director, and Betty was selected because, as General Mill says, it has a "warm and friendly sound." The famous signature is the result of a contest held among women employees. **7. Real.** Mama Celeste is Celeste Lizio of Wheaton, Ill., who began by selling her frozen pizzas made in her Chicago restaurant, established in 1937. She remains a consultant to Quaker Oats Co., which bought Mama Celeste in 1969. **8. Real.** Dr. Charles Pepper of Rural Retreat, Va., had a lovely daughter. W. B. Morrison, owner of an old corner drugstore in Waco, Texas, was infatuated with her and suggested that the inventor of the drink, Charles Alderton, a pharmacist in his store, name the fluid for the belle's father. Alas, W. B. Morrison never achieved more than her father's name. **9. Real.** Jack Newton Daniel (not Daniels) was the founder of the distillery. **10. Real.** Philip Morris was tobacconist on London's Bond Street nearly 100 years ago. He is not to be confused with Johnny, the real midget bellhop Johnny Rovatini, who became the voice and symbol for the company and is now retired.

Source: Quiz by Carol Posten. Reprinted with permission from *Advertising Age*, May 24, 1982. Copyright © 1982 by Crain Communications.

Democracy—Corporate Style
(Or Someone Out There Doesn't Like Vernon Jordan)

When R. J. Reynolds Industries, the nation's largest cigarette maker, held its annual meeting in Wilmington, Delaware, on April 28, 1982, here's how the voting for directors turned out (a total of 104,381,024 shares of common stock were entitled to vote):

	VOTES		
Joseph F. Abely, Jr.	87,458,041	Juanita M. Kreps	87,336,833
William S. Anderson	87,437,215	Richard G. Landis	87,454,658
Albert L. Butler, Jr.	87,445,809	John D. Macomber	87,453,448
Herschel H. Cudd	87,445,737	H. C. Roemer	87,424,457
Ronald H. Grierson	87,459,697	J. Paul Sticht	87,421,001
John W. Hanley	87,442,593	Colin Stokes	87,414,191
Edward A. Horrigan, Jr.	87,459,113	J. Tylee Wilson	87,462,389
Jerome W. Hull	87,432,883	Margaret S. Wilson	87,443,360
Vernon E. Jordan, Jr.	87,204,731		

The Only Head of a Major U.S. Company Who Was Born in New Zealand

Keith Crane, Colgate-Palmolive.

The Ms. Three

Celebrating its 10th birthday in 1982, *Ms.* magazine saluted 36 "men who've taken chances and made a difference" in opening opportunities for women. Three were from the business world:

Coy Eklund, chairman of Equitable Life Assurance

Ron Moss, chairman of the ad agency Kenyon & Ekchardt

David Mitchell, chairman of Avon Products

Mr. Bounderby

Charles Dickens' description of the typical businessman, Mr. Bounderby, in his 1854 novel, *Hard Times:*

He was a rich man: banker, merchant, manufacturer, and what not. A big, loud man, with a stare, and a metallic laugh. A man made out of a coarse material, which seemed to have been stretched to make so much of him. A man with a great puffed head and forehead, swelled veins in his temples, and such a strained skin to his face that it seemed to hold his eyes opend, and lift his eyebrows up. A man with a pervading appearance on him of being inflated like a balloon, and ready to start. A man who could never sufficiently vaunt himself a self-made man. A man who was always proclaiming through that brassy speaking-trumpet of a voice of his, his old ignorance and his old poverty. A man who was the Bully of humility.

Thanks, Dad

Company chiefs who hold the position once held by their fathers:

Steve Bechtel, Jr., Bechtel

W. L. Lyons Brown, Jr., Brown-Forman

August A. Busch III, Anheuser-Busch

Otis Chandler, *Times-Mirror*

A. Dano Davis, Winn-Dixie

Richard Gelb, Bristol-Myers

Avram J. Goldberg, Stop & Shop (actually, father-in-law)

J. Peter Grace, W. R. Grace

Katharine Graham, *Washington Post*

Donald Hall, Hallmark

Christie Hefner, Playboy Enterprises

William Hewitt, John Deere (father-in-law)

Barron Hilton, Hilton Hotels

Joseph R. Hyde III, Malone & Hyde

Marshall P. Katz, Papercraft

Arthur D. Little, Narragansett Capital

Robert M. Long, Longs Drug Stores

Peter A. Magowan, Safeway Stores

Richard A. Manoogian, Masco

J. Willard Marriott, Jr., Marriott

Forrest E. Mars, Jr. and John F. Mars, Mars

Sanford McDonnell, McDonnell-Douglas (actually, uncle)

Harold W. McGraw, Jr. McGraw-Hill

S. I. Newhouse and Donald Newhouse, Advance Publications (Newhouse)

Arthur C. Nielsen, A. C. Nielsen

Ray T. Parfet, Jr., Upjohn (father-in-law)

Clement Stone, Combined International

Arthur O. Sulzberger, *New York Times*

Donald and Robert Taicher, Caressa

R. Lee Taylor II, Feeral Company

William R. Timken, Timken

George H. Weyerhaeuser, Weyerhaeuser

William Wrigley, Wm. Wrigley, Jr.

Employee Stake in the Company

Percentage of company's shares held by employee stock ownership plans (ESOPs) or profit-sharing programs:

Chicago & Northwestern Transportation	57.0%	McGraw-Edison	15.0%
Donaldson, Lufkin & Jenrette	50.0%	Stone & Webster	14.4%
Grumman	50.0%	Armco	14.0%
L. S. Starret	50.0%	Logicon	14.0%
FMC	33.9%	Varo	14.0%
Allied Products	31.0%	Ford Motor	13.8%
Cooper Tire & Rubber	27.0%	Burlington Industries	13.0%
Products Resources & Chemicals	27.0%	Federal Mogul	12.0%
Parsons	26.0%	TRW	10.5%
Lowe's Companies	25.0%	GenRad	10.0%
Northop	25.0%	Federated Department Stores	9.7%
Thrifty	24.9%	Crown Cork & Seal	8.0%
Sears, Roebuck	22.5%	Gerber Products	7.7%
Textron	20.0%	Wurlitzer	7.0%
Carter Hawley Hale	18.5%	Chris-Craft	6.8%
Conwood	18.0%	Phillips Petroleum	6.7%
DeSoto	17.3%	Procter & Gamble	5.8%
Elgin National	17.0%	Marion Labs	5.7%
Bell & Howell	15.3%	Abbott Labs	5.5%
Tandy	15.2%	Kaiser Steel	5.2%
American Agronomics	15.0%	AT&T	2.2%
Anthony Industries	15.0%		

Source: Salomon Brothers.

John F. Welch, Jr.

Jack Welch is the youngest chief executive officer (CEO) in the history of General Electric. When he took over on April 1, 1981, he was 45. He was handpicked by his predecessor, Reginald Jones, who apparently preferred someone young and energetic for the trying years ahead. Jones described Welch as the "prototype of the chief executive officer of the 1980s."

Welch is a desk-pounder who wants to instill in the GE troops (there are 400,000 of them) a sense of urgency. It's the way he was during his climb up the GE ladder. When he became a GE group manager, he had a special telephone line installed in his office with a private number known only to his purchasing agents. Anytime an agent got a price concession from a supplier, he would call Welch with the news. Welch would interrupt any meeting to take the call and congratulate the agent, saying something like, "That's wonderful news, you just knocked a nickel per ton off the price of steel." And then he would follow it up with a handwritten note of congratulations. Today, Jack Welch is telling his top managers that he wants GE to be first or second in all the businesses the company competes in—and that's 250 businesses—or else get out of the business.

Welch is also the first Ph.D. to head the company. The son of a railroad conductor, Welch grew up in Salem, Massachusetts, not far from the GE town of Lynn. In high school he was captain of both the golf and hockey teams. He became a chemical engineer at the University of Massachusetts and took his advanced degrees—M.S. and Ph.D.—at the University of Illinois. When he joined GE in 1960, shortly after he married the former Carolyn Osburn, his first assignment was back in his native state at GE's chemical development facility in Pittsfield. He, like most GE managers, has never worked for another company. Welch's stepping stone to the top was a new GE business: engineered plastics (Lexan, Noryl).

Presiding at his first annual meeting, Welch told shareholders that while GE already has a good reputation, he's pushing the company to improve to the point where "in the world's assessment" GE's quality and excellence "are not issues for conjecture, but indisputable facts."

Don't think you can just sit back and take it easy because you work for a big company. At GE, Jack Welch won't let you. Welch was paid $859,000 in 1981. The Welches have four children—two boys, two girls.

Roberto C. Goizueta

Coca-Cola has always been a rather inbred company, and so although it's big, many people on the outside (and even some on the inside) don't know what goes on there. It therefore surprised many observers when, in 1980, Cuban-born Roberto C. Goizueta became president and then, a year later, chairman and chief executive officer—at age 49. Goizeuta contrasts sharply with J. Paul Austin, the aloof lawyer who formerly ran the company. He's warm and outgoing, he likes to wear silk ascots and dark glasses, and he even talks to the press—and, once in a while, to security analysts. "Neither the boss nor the CEO should be treated as God," is a Goizuetism.

Goizueta was born in Havana, but went to prep school in the United States and then to Yale before returning home, where he answered a blind newspaper ad for a bilingual chemist. The year was 1954, the job turned out to be with Coca-Cola-Cuba—and Goizeuta has never been with another company. Coke transferred him to Nassau as Caribbean-area chemist after Fidel Castro took over the island.

Goizeuta is having a lot of fun shaking up Coke. Goizueta forced the company's longtime ad agency, McCann-Erickson, to take on a veteran Pepsi-Cola adman as head of the Coke account. He went out and had Coke buy Columbia Pictures, explaining jokingly that Columbia's top management "dresses as conservatively—if not more so—than I do." And he approved extension of the valued Coke name to a new product, Diet Coke, which he introduced in New York City at a one-night $100,000 publicity extravanganza. Yes, Roberto Goizueta is something else. The Wall Street Journal said the most impressive part of his performance was his ability to get approval from Coke's conservative board of directors. "It's simply a matter of showing them the facts, of being very open," explained Goizueta. "I tell them, 'You know, we are never going to beat Pepsi-Cola in Chicago unless we do something about it.'" Watch for Coke to do something in Chicago, long a Pepsi stronghold.

Goizueta and his wife, the former Olga Castaleiro, have lived for many years in the same modest house in Atlanta. They have three children, Roberto, Olga Maria (Mrs. Thompson T. Rawls II), and Javier.

Goizeuta's compensation in 1981: $1 million.

Philip Caldwell

On October 1, 1979, Ford Motor Company did something unprecedented. For the first time in its 73-year history it named a non-Ford to head the company. He was white-haired Philip Caldwell, who had spent 26 years with Ford, steadily climbing the managerial rungs. He first made his mark as head of trucks; he breathed life back into the old Philco unit; he introduced the Fiesta in Europe.

Caldwell's father died when Philip was young, leaving his mother, Wilhelmina, a high school librarian, to bring up four boys. She did, sending all of them to college during the Depression. College for Phil Caldwell was Muskingum, a small Ohio institution affiliated with the United Presbyterian church. He went on to get an M.B.A. from the prestigious Harvard Business School before entering the Navy in 1942.

After World War II, Caldwell remained with the Navy as a civilian employee in procurement, where he did so well that in 1950 he was given the William A. Jump award given annually to the federal employee under 32 with the most outstanding performance in public administration. In 1953, at the suggestion of a Navy colleague, he joined Ford in procurement, which has to do with the purchase of supplies from outsiders.

Caldwell would seem to be the polar opposite of the man who everyone thought might succeed Henry Ford II one day—flamboyant Lee A. Iacocca, who was fired in 1979 when Ford called him in and told him, "I just don't like you." Iacocca then became head of Chrysler, taking with him a lot of Ford people, and Caldwell moved into position at Ford. People who work with him describe Caldwell as "the ultimate manager, tremendously well-organized and very precise." He and his wife, Betsy, live in the fancy Detroit suburb of Bloomfield Hills. They have three children. One of Phil Caldwell's passions in life is collecting antiques. Asked once to depict his management philosophy, he said: "The idea is not to have home runs. The idea is to win the game and win the pennant above all. So a dazzling home run is interesting and attractive. But at the end of the day you'd like to have won the pennant. That suggests that the teamwork approach is a good one."

In 1981, when Ford lost $1 billion, eliminating bonuses, Caldwell earned $450,000.

The Women Directors

Fifteen years ago fewer than fifty women served on boards of major corporations—and these were mostly related to founders or heads of the companies. Today, some four hundred companies have female directors. One-third of the *Fortune* 500 has a woman on the board. The following ten women sit on at least five boards:

Anne L. Armstrong, former Ambassador to the Court of St. James's: Boise Cascade, General Foods, General Motors, First City Bancorp of Texas, Braniff International.

Catherine B. Cleary, adjunct professor, School of Business Administration, University of Wisconsin, Milwaukee: Dart & Kraft, General Motors, First Wisconsin Trust, Northwestern Mutual Life Insurance, American Telephone & Telegraph.

Joan Ganz Cooney, president, Children's Television Workshop: Johnson & Johnson, Xerox, First Pennsylvania Corporation, May Department Stores, Metropolitan Life Insurance.

Martha W. Griffiths, former Michigan congresswoman: Burroughs, Chrysler, Greyhound, Consumers Power Company, K mart.

Carla Anderson Hills, former Housing and Urban Development Secretary, now an attorney: Standard Oil of California, IBM, The Signal Companies, Corning Glass Works, American Airlines.

Juanita M. Kreps, former U.S. Secretary of Commerce: Eastman Kodak, R. J. Reynolds Industries, United Airlines, Citicorp, J. C. Penney, AT&T.

Jewel S. Lafontant, attorney, former U.S. Solicitor General: Mobil Oil, Bendix, Harte-Hanks Communications, Continental Illinois, Trans World Airlines, Equitable Life Assurance, Foote, Cone & Belding.

Patricia O'Donnell Shontz Longe, economist, Graduate School of Business Administration, University of Michigan: American Motors, Detroit Edison, Kroger, Manufacturers National, Warner Lambert.

Gertrude G. Michelson, senior vice president, external affairs, R. H. Macy & Co., New York: General Electric, Goodyear Tire & Rubber, Quaker Oats, Stanley Works, Chubb, Harper & Row.

Norma T. Pace, economist, vice president, American Paper Institute: 3M, Sperry Corproation, Milton Bradley Company, Chase Manhattan, Sears, Reobuck.

Sources: *Catalyst; Business & Society Review.*

The 16 Best Places for Women to Work

American Express	Equitable Life Assurance Society
Atlantic Richfield	General Mills
American Telephone & Telegraph	Hewlett-Packard
Chemical Bank	Honeywell
Connecticut General (now part of CIGNA)	IBM
Continental Illinois Bank	Johnson & Johnson
Control Data	Quaker Oats
Digital Equipment Corp.	Security Pacific Bank Source: *Savvy.*

The 21 Club: Corporate Chiefs Paid More Than $2 Million in 1981

		Company	Salary*
1.	STEVEN J. ROSS	Warner Communications	$1,954,136
2.	CHARLES LAZARUS	Toys 'R' Us	$1,223,122
3.	GEORGE PLATT	Texas International	$640,232
4.	FRANK G. HICKEY	General Instrument	$623,955
5.	DAVID TENDLER	Phibro	$2,125,000
6.	GEORGE T. SCHARFFENBERGER	City Investing	$843,500
7.	JAMES H. EVANS	Union Pacific	$953,661
8.	DEAN L. BUNTROCK	Waste Management	$523,808
9.	JOHN V. JAMES	Dresser Industries	$377,651
10.	AUGUST A. BUSCH III	Anheuser-Busch	$729,950
11.	ROBERT T. GROHMAN	Levi Strauss	$401,000
12.	ROBERT ANDERSON	Rockwell International	$1,115,000
13.	THOMAS R. WILCOX	Crocker National Bank	$432,000
14.	MAURICE R. GREENBERG	American International Group	$476,000
15.	HERBERT C. CORNUELLE	Dillingham	$510,000
16.	FRED L. HARTLEY	Union Oil of California	$1,300,000
17.	J. PETER GRACE	W. R. Grace	$1,486,000
18.	J. HUGH LIEDTKE	Pennzoil	$562,000
19.	DAVID S. LEWIS	General Dynamics	$420,000
20.	DONALD H. RUMSFELD	G. D. Searle	$586,000
21.	JAMES R. LESCH	Hughes Tool	$501,000

The Year for Bankruptcies

1982 turned out to be a terrific year for bankruptcies. Dun & Bradstreet, the grim reaper of these statistics, reported that in the week ended August 26, business bankruptcies reached a level not seen since the Depression year of 1933: 696.

In the first 44 weeks of 1982, business failures totaled 21,597, or an average of 491 per week. That was up 50% over the 1981 level.

Among the major corporations that filed during the year for protection under Chapter 11 of the Federal Bankruptcy laws were:

MANVILLE (Formerly Johns-Manville)

REVERE COPPER & BRASS

WICKES

SAXON INDUSTRIES

BRANIFF INTERNATIONAL

10 Best Places for Blacks to Work

American Telephone & Telegraph

Equitable Life Assurance

Exxon

Gannett

General Electric

General Motors

Hewlett-Packard

IBM

Sea-Land (subsidiary of R. J. Reynolds)

Xerox

Source: *Black Enterprise.*

Stock Gains**	Total Income***
$19,421,142	$22,554,410
$6,334,200	$7,613,004
$5,863,000	$6,631,302
$5,636,839	$5,269,250
$1,161,875	$3,830,381
$2,414,704	$3,416,660
$1,863,100	$2,835,731
$2,186,859	$2,828,989
$1,063,902	$2,640,223
$1,896,350	$2,630,930
$1,265,000	$2,484,000
$981,000	$2,438,000
$1,911,000	$2,405,000
$1,876,000	$2,355,000
$1,420,000	$2,341,000
$798,000	$2,340,000
$523,000	$2,333,000
$1,218,000	$2,229,000
$1,699,000	$2,194,000
$1,102,000	$2,182,000
$1,334,000	$2,052,000

*Salary includes salary payments, cash bonuses, and director's fees.

**Stock gains represent the difference between what the executive paid for stock and its actual market price. Thus if he were given the right (option) to purchase 100 shares at $20 per share in 1979 and decided to exercise that option in 1981 when the stock was selling for $50 per share, his stock gain would be $30 per share, or $3,000 from the transaction.

***Total Income includes salary, stock gains, contingent remuneration (amounts deferred for payment at a later time), and benefits (such as company-paid life insurance premiums, use of company car or plane, club dues, and other fringes).

Source: Reprinted by permission of *Forbes,* from the June 7, 1982, issue. Copyright © 1982 Forbes Inc.

One Big Happy Family

Warner Communications

Mad magazines

New York Cosmos soccer team

Atari computers

One Big Happy Family

Greyhound

Greyhound Bus Lines
Dial soap
Armour hot dogs

The Babson 22

The Academy of Distinguished Entrepreneurs was established at Boston's Babson College in 1977 to recognize men and women who had "both the vision and tenacity to build their own successful ventures" and who "have contributed significantly and in a socially positive direction to the development of free enterprise throughout the world." A board of editors and publishers, including Robert L. Bartley of the Wall Street Journal, *Malcolm S. Forbes, Jr., of* Forbes, *and Andrew Neil of* The Economist, *select the people for induction into the Academy. So far (through 1982) 22 have been chosen. The selections, year by year, were:*

1978: **Kenneth H. Olsen,** Digital Equipment Corp.
      Berry Gordy, Motown Industries
      Soichiro Honda, Honda Motor
      Ray Kroc, McDonald's
      Royal Little, Textron

1979: **John H. Johnson,** Johnson Publishing
      Byung-Chull Lee, Samsung Group (South Korea)
      Diane Von Furstenberg, DVF Inc.
      John Erik Jonsson, Texas Instruments
      Thomas Mellon Evans, Crane Company

1980: **J. Peter Grace,** W. R. Grace
      Mary Hudson, Hudson Oil
      Mary Wells Lawrence, Wells, Rich, Greene
      Lewis E. Lehrman, Rite Aid Corp.

1981: **Franklin P. Perdue,** Perdue Farms
      Gustavo A. Cisneros, Organizacion Diego Cisneros
      An Wang, Wang Laboratories
      Marcus Wallenberg, Skandinavisk-Enskilda Banken (Sweden)

1982: **Wally Amos,** Famous Amos Chocolate Chip Cookie
      Armand Hammer, Occidental Petroleum
      William C. Norris, Control Data
      Carl G. Sontheimer, Cuisinarts Inc.

Business Hall of Famers

There was no Business Hall of Fame until 1975 when the Junior Achievement organization established one. Why? Junior Achievement explained:

"We in America are forever heaping attention, praise, recognition, awards, and even huge sums of money on movie stars, TV celebrities, athletes, politicians, authors, and scientists.

"But, we seem unwilling or unable to acknowledge that outstanding business achievements demand talent, brains, sensitivity, education, training, and a sense of leadership—not unlike some of the fields of endeavor which regularly receive our acclaim."

So into that breach stepped Junior Achievement. It got Fortune's *board of editors to agree to select the laureates—and presto, the National Business Hall of Fame was in business.*

Nineteen were admitted to the Hall in the first year, and more were elected each following year. Through 1982, the Business Hall of Fame had admitted 75 members.

Here they are, year by year:

1975 Laureates

HENRY FORD (1863–1947)

Henry Ford didn't invent the automobile, but he did invent the mass-production technique that enabled the average Joe to buy a Ford Model T for as little as $260. The Model T became the first mass-produced auto in 1913. A year later, he doubled wages to $5 a day so that workers could afford to buy the cars they were producing.

JOHN D. ROCKEFELLER (1839–1937)

The son of a strict Calvinist mother and a con artist father, John D. Rockefeller was the acknowledged founder of what we now know as the petroleum industry, using tactics that helped to give the late nineteenth century its "robber baron" image. He rode roughshod over competitors, squeezing them out, and by 1880 he controlled 95% of the country's oil. Later he became a great philanthropist. The Supreme Court broke up his Trust in 1911, but his "mother" company survives today as Exxon, the world's largest corporation.

J. PIERPONT MORGAN (1837–1913)

J. P. Morgan was a brilliant mathematician (he studied at the University of Göttingen in Germany) who applied his skill at numbers to financing and organizing giant corporations—U.S. Steel, International Nickel, General Electric—at the dawn of the U.S. industrial age. Morgan loans once saved the U.S. government—and Harper & Row—from bankruptcy.

ALFRED P. SLOAN, JR. (1875–1966)

An MIT-trained engineer, Sloan was the architect of GM's decentralized management structure. Under his leadership GM wrested first place in the auto industry from Ford. His book, *My Years with General Motors,* is a textbook on how to run a big corporation.

A. P. GIANNINI (1870–1949)

Born to Italian immigrants in San Jose, California, Amadeo Peter Giannini started the Bank of Italy in San Francisco's North Beach district to serve the "little fellow." He put branches all over the state of California and lived to see his bank, now the Bank of America, become the world's largest, much to the chagrin of eastern bankers, who tried more than once to undo him. (1982 marked the first time the Bank of America did not have on its board a director of Italian ancestry.)

GEORGE WASHINGTON (1732–1799)

The "Father of our country" could also be counted among the fathers of agribusiness. On his Mount Vernon farm George Washington calculated yields per acre, the most efficient farm animals, divisions of labor for harvest, and crops that increased land productivity.

ELI WHITNEY (1765–1825)

Eli Whitney's cotton gin enabled one operator to clean as many seeds out of cotton as 50 workers could do by hand. It made cotton the South's biggest cash crop. Later, Whitney invented a way to mass-produce muskets with interchangeable parts, paving the way for the industrial factories of the North.

CYRUS H. MCCORMICK (1809–1884)

His reaper could cut ten acres of wheat a day compared to the one-and-one-half a man with a scythe could handle. But Cyrus McCormick was more than a mechanical inventor. He pioneered such marketing techniques as money-back guarantees and paying on the installment plan through his company, the forerunner of International Harvester.

ANDREW CARNEGIE (1835–1919)

Scottish-born Andrew Carnegie saved his money, invested wisely, and by application of strict cost accounting built the largest steel company in America. Wall Streeters called him the "Scotch pirate." At the turn of the century, he sold Carnegie Steel to J. P. Morgan for $480 million and spent the rest of his life giving away money, notably for the establishment of 2,500 public libraries across the country.

THEODORE N. VAIL (1845–1920)

Putting together a monopoly is one thing. Making it run well is something else. That was Theodore Vail's contribution. There may not have been a Bell Telephone

System, at least not as we know it, without the managerial skills of Vail, who never went beyond high school. He fashioned American Telephone & Telegraph (AT&T), now ticketed for dismemberment.

ALEXANDER T. STEWART (1803–1876)

Irish-born Alexander Stewart parlayed a $5,000 inheritance into the fabulous Marble Palace at Broadway and Chambers Street in New York. The prototype of the modern department store, it had set prices (no haggling), toilets, free delivery, and seasonal clearances. For many years, one-tenth of all the goods entering the Port of New York went to the Marble Palace.

THOMAS A. EDISON(1847–1931)

Probably the most famous of all inventors, Thomas Edison held 1,098 patents, including the electric light, phonograph, and movie projector. When the Morgan Bank combined his Edison Electric Light with a competitor to form General Electric in 1892, Edison was annoyed that his name no longer headed the company. He refused to "go on the board of a company that I don't control."

J. EDGAR THOMSON (1808–1874)

An engineer like his father, Edgar Thomson became president of the Pennsylvania Railroad in 1852. During his 22-year presidency he cut costs, substituted steel rails for iron, expanded trackage from 250 to 6,000 miles, and built the Pennsy into the country's first great railroad.

DAVID SARNOFF (1891–1971)

David Sarnoff was the Morse Code operator who, in 1912, received the weak signal: "*S.S. Titanic* ran into iceberg. Sinking fast." When Radio Corporation of America (at the behest of the U.S. government) took over the British-owned Marconi Company, Sarnoff emerged as the general manager. He produced the first sports broadcast in 1921 (the Dempsey vs. Carpentier fight). He made radios, and he formed NBC to supply radio programs. Later he made RCA into the pioneer manufacturer of television sets.

GEORGE EASTMAN (1854–1932)

George Eastman was a Rochester, New York, bank clerk before he turned his talents to inventing a dry plate that would eliminate cumbersome camera equipment. In 1900, his company, Eastman Kodak, was selling a $1 Brownie camera and a roll of six films for 15¢. His philosophy always was to put inexpensive, easy-to-use cameras into the hands of amateurs who would then take a lot of pictures which Kodak would develop. In 1932, at age 77, Eastman asked his doctor where his heart was and then shot himself, leaving a note: "To my friends. My work is done. Why wait?"

M. J. RATHBONE (1900–1976)

Who foresaw the OPEC stranglehold on oil back in the petroleum-rich 1960s? Exxon today owns more reserves outside the Middle East than any other large oil company, thanks to the foresight of Monroe J. Rathbone, an engineer who headed the company from 1960 to 1965 and who convinced the board to spend $700 million to find more oil.

J. ERIK JONSSON (1901–   )

The transistor was invented at Bell Laboratories, but it was Texas Instruments, deep in the heart of Texas, that first learned how to mass-produce the thin energy conductor that revolutionized the electronics industry. Then at the helm of T. I. was Erik Jonsson, a Brooklyn-born Rensselaer engineer who helped to create one of the biggest corporations to emerge after World War II. After retiring, he was elected mayor of Dallas.

WILLIAM M. ALLEN (1900–   )

The end of a war is not a good time to be the head of an airplane manufacturer. But Boeing's William Allen, a lawyer, not only kept his company in business, he plunked down $20 million, with no customers in sight, to build the first American jetliner, the 707. It was the crucial move in ushering Boeing into the dominant position in the world aircraft industry.

ROYAL LITTLE (1896–   )

Royal Little, nephew of the pioneer consultant Arthur D. Little, is regarded as the father of the conglomerate. He pushed an old New England textile company, Textron, into what he called "unrelated diversification" because it just wasn't doing well, even after deserting New England for the nonunionized factories of the South. Textron companies make helicopters, chainsaws, staplers, watchbands, lawn mowers, and bearings, among other products.

1976 Laureates

CHARLES EDWARD MERRILL (1885–1956)

Charles Merrill believed in "people's capitalism." So, with his partner Edmund Lynch, he opened a stock brokerage house, establishing offices throughout the country to encourage small investors to put money into the stock market. He was also a founder of Safeway Stores.

ALBERT DAVIS LASKER (1880–1952)

Lasker boasted that he made "more money out of advertising than any man who ever lived." His ad campaigns popularized Puffed Wheat and Puffed Rice, Kotex, Kleenex, and Lucky Strikes. He passed his firm on to three associates, Foote, Cone, and Belding.

JAMES JEROME HILL (1838–1916)

Hill saw a lot more with his one eye than most people see with two. He saw the need for transportation to the deserted Northwest. His Great Northern railroad almost single-handedly populated the Northwest, carrying farmers, lumberjacks, and businessmen to Minnesota, Montana, Idaho, and Washington.

THOMAS JOHN WATSON, JR. (1914–   )

Watson's father created International Business Machines out of the Computer-Tabulating-Recording Co. But it was Tom Jr. who moved IBM into the computer age. When Remington Rand came out with the UNIVAC computer in 1951, Watson pushed his IBM research and sales teams into a leadership position they never relinquished. He made IBM synonymous with the computer.

WILLIAM COOPER PROCTER (1862–1934)

Back from Princeton in 1883, Cooper Procter joined the soapmaking company cofounded by his grandfather 46 years earlier. It was already a successful enterprise, and Procter made it even stronger by building into its operations a concern for employees. In 1885, he shortened the workweek to five and one-half days. In 1887, he established a profit-sharing plan. Later he guaranteed most P&G employees 48 weeks of work every year. After his death, P&G employees put up a memorial to him in Cincinnati.

JAMES CASH PENNEY (1875–1971)

J. C. Penney, the son of a lay Primitive Baptist preacher, who taught him a rigorous social ethic, believed in the Golden Rule. Penney's Golden Rule stores, later called J. C. Penney, quickly multiplied through the West, thanks to his policy of giving store managers a cut of the profits. He called his employees "partners" and "associates." He loved being known as "the man with a thousand partners."

GEORGE STEVENS MOORE (1905–   )

Citicorp chairman Walter Wriston credits George Moore with "the fastest financial mind in existence." As president of New York's First National City Bank (now Citicorp), Moore was largely responsible for moving American banking into two new fields—diversified financial services (real estate, factoring, leasing) and overseas banking (Citibank now has branches in 104 countries).

STEPHEN DAVISON BECHTEL, SR. (1900–   )

Steve Bechtel grew up in the on-site construction camps his father set up. Then he and his two brothers turned their family enterprise into the biggest construction and engineering firm in the world, doing mammoth jobs—Hoover Dam, San Francisco Bay Bridge, the emerging city of Jubail in Saudi Arabia—for government customers.

WALTER ELIAS DISNEY (1901–1966)

The world's most famous animator, he couldn't draw his Mickey Mouse or other beloved Disney cartoon characters. But he had big ideas and the ability to set them in motion. *Snow White and the Seven Dwarfs,* the first feature-length cartoon, became a smash hit in 1937. He won Oscar after Oscar with *Fantasia, Pinocchio, Peter Pan* and, in the fifties, live action movies. He conquered television with *The Mickey Mouse Club* and *Disney's Wonderful World*. With Disneyland, he set his super-clean image of American wholesomeness on that seedy American institution, the amusement park.

CYRUS ROWLETT SMITH (1899–

C. R. Smith, a Texan who headed American Airlines from 1934 to 1968, marketed flying "like a box of Post Toasties." To alleviate passengers' fears, her wrote the famed ad of 1937, "Afraid to Fly?" He made American Airlines number one by 1940. A workaholic, Smith spared only four days for a honeymoon after he was married. His wife later divorced him.

1977 Laureates

BENJAMIN FRANKLIN (1706–1790)

Ben Franklin followed his nose to an occupation. He didn't care for the smell of tallow in his father's Boston candle shop. Ink was his perfume. He published his famous best-seller, *Poor Richard's Almanac,* as well as the Pennsylvania *Gazette,* at his print shop in Philadelphia. He left the business world at 42, a well-off man, to turn his thoughts to scientific experiments, revolutionary activity, international diplomacy, and government service. Poor Richard's sayings continued to shape the consciousness of American businessmen for nearly 250 years.

HENRY ROBINSON LUCE(1898–1967)

The son of a missionary to China, Henry Luce became the father of the modern American magazine. "Timestyle," the punchy prose style of *Time,* changed the voice of American journalism. *Life* virtually created the genre of photojournalism. *Fortune* brought literary quality to business reporting, as did *Sports Illustrated* to sports journalism.

ROBERT WINSHIP WOODRUFF (1890–   )

A share of Coca-Cola stock worth $75 in 1923, when Woodruff took over, would now be worth some $10,000. He did it by instilling his vision of Coke as something more than a soft drink. To Woodruff, selling Coca-Cola was selling a wholesome image; indeed, it's a symbol of America to millions of people throughout the world.

JOHN JAY MCCLOY (1895–   )

He's known on Wall Street as "the head of the Establishment," exemplifying the close ties between government and business. As chairman of the Chase National Bank, he managed the merger that brought the one-time "banker's bank" into retail banking; today's Chase has dozens of branches throughout New York City. He served as assistant secretary of war under Roosevelt, high commissioner for Germany under Truman, and disarmament advisor to Kennedy.

WILLIAM BLACKIE (1907–   )

Not too many boys say, "I want to be a businessman when I grow up," but that's supposedly what Blackie told his parents as a child in Glasgow, Scotland. He moved to Chicago and joined Caterpillar Tractor in 1939. He preached that foreign investment created jobs here. Under his direction, Caterpillar built plants around the world. Caterpillar's exports also increased greatly, and the company still ranks as one of America's biggest exporters year after year.

JOYCE CLYDE HALL (1891–1982)

It was Joyce Hall who realized that when people send a greeting card, they don't want it to be tacky. He built the world's largest greeting card company on the concept, "Good Taste is Good Business." He died on Oct. 29, 1982.

HENRY JOHN KAISER (1882–1967)

Kaiser brought industry to the West. His West Coast shipyards attracted thousands of workers during the Second World War; his steel mill near Los Angeles was the first west of the Mississippi; his cement plant in California, was the largest in the world; his aluminum plants in the Northwest changed the nature of that region's workforce. Like many Westerners, Kaiser was a maverick industrialist. A New Deal Democrat, he launched a comprehensive health care plan in which three million people are enrolled today.

FLORENCE NIGHTINGALE GRAHAM (1878–1966)

As Florence Nightingale Graham she worked as a nurse for three weeks. As Elizabeth Arden, opening her first beauty salon on Fifth Avenue in 1910, she reigned as queen of the beauty industry for over 50 years. The company that bears her name is now owned by the stuffy pharmaceutical house Eli Lilly.

1978 Laureates

HENRY JOHN HEINZ (1844–1919)

The product of a strict Lutheran household, Heinz founded a food processing company that was basically an extension of the work he did as a boy—bottling and selling condiments made from the yield of a kitchen garden. Teddy Roosevelt once gave Heinz a hearty "bully bully" for being one of the few food processors to support federal pure food laws. He was one of the first American businessmen to sell abroad, making his name a household word in Britain.

FREDERICK WEYERHAEUSER (1834–1914)

By the time he died, Weyerhaeuser had bought almost 2 million acres of Northwest forestland at an average cost of $8.80 an acre. A German immigrant, Weyerhaeuser always seemed to be in the right place at the right time. He was a neighbor of railroad magnate James J. Hill in St. Paul when Hill decided to sell him 900,000 acres of land. His forest products company is still run by his descendants.

DONALD WILLS DOUGLAS (1892–1982)

A pioneer plane builder, Douglas made aviation history with the DC-3, whose metal frame and comfortable interior made commercial air travel a reality. During World War II, Douglas built nearly 30,000 planes (10,000 of them DC-3s) in what *Fortune* called "one of the great feats of modern industrial history." The son of a Brooklyn bank cashier, Douglas studied at MIT to become one of the first aeronautical engineers. His failure to come up with a jet airliner to match Boeing's 707 eventually cost his company its independence.

HARRY BLAIR CUNNINGHAM (1907–   )

An ex-newspaperman, Cunningham understood the significance of the move to the suburbs by millions of Americans during the 1950s. He launched the first K-mart discount chain in 1962, thereby transforming his company, S. S. Kresge, from an also-ran in retailing to the hottest competitor of industry giant Sears, Roebuck.

JOSEPH IRWIN MILLER (1909–   )

Descended from a family of ministers and successful businessmen, Joseph Miller returned from Yale and Oxford to take the helm at Cummins Engine in 1934, building it, over the next 40 years, into the nation's largest maker of diesel engines for trucks. An ethicist, he desegregated both his company and his hometown, Columbus, Indiana. He also transformed Columbus into an oasis in the Midwest by hiring the most distinguished architects in the nation to design the town's public buildings.

CONRAD NICHOLSON HILTON (1887–1979)

"There is no such thing as being a little enthusiastic," Hilton used to say. His enthusiasm carried him from humble beginnings, renting out rooms in the family house in New Mexico, to a chain of hotels in the United States and abroad, including New York's Waldorf-Astoria.

ARTHUR VINING DAVIS (1867–1962)

Charles Martin Hall finally figured out a cheap way to separate aluminum from its oxide in 1885. Arthur Davis, a young Amherst graduate who helped pour the ingot at the Pittsburgh Reduction, came up with the first practical use of aluminum—pots. Davis convinced banker Andrew Mellon to back the company, Aluminum Company of American or Alcoa. It was the start of the aluminum industry.

FRANCIS CABOT LOWELL (1775–1817)

Lowell was one of the earliest industrial spies. While in Scotland to improve his health, he toured textile mills where the power looms were a technological secret. But Lowell, a former Harvard mathematician, stored in his photographic memory all the mechanical information necessary to reconstruct the looms back in America. The mills he founded at Waltham, Massachusetts, formed the basis of the American textile industry.

1979 Laureates

ROSWELL GARST (1898–1977)

Roswell Garst was a missionary of modern, efficient agriculture. He traveled thousands of miles of dirt roads in the 1930s, getting farmers to plant the hybrid corn developed by his friend Henry A. Wallace. He was an early supporter of chemical fertilizers, synthetic protein, and trade with Russia. He and his wife, Elizabeth Garst, worked as a team—and it was Mrs. Garst's invitation that got Nikita Khrushchev (and his wife) to insist on visiting the Garst farm in Coon Rapids, Iowa. When Garst died, the family had a $50-million-a-year seed business and a cattle herd of 4,000.

JOHN HENRY PATTERSON (1844–1922)

The "autocrat of the cash register" was a tough, tyrannical master of the hard sell. He terrorized his sales force to sell the cash register into stores everywhere. He regarded competitors as beneath contempt. He built the biggest company in

Dayton, Ohio: National Cash Register (now NCR). IBM founder Thomas Watson, who worked at National Cash, once described Patterson as "an amalgam of St. Paul, Poor Richard, and Adolf Hitler."

CORNELIUS VANDERBILT (1794–1877)

Transportation was Commodore Vanderbilt's game. At age 16 he started a ferryboat service from Staten Island to Manhattan. Then he entered the shipping business, designing his own vessels (he was also adept at piloting them). Finally, at age 68, he embraced railroading, eventually gaining control of the New York Central. He made $100 million, some of which he relinquished after the Civil War to start the college in Nashville that bears his name.

ROBERT ELKINGTON WOOD (1879–1969)

Having read the *Statistical Abstract of the United States* for fun, General Wood deduced that mail-order customers—the farmers—would soon be moving to the city. He quit Montgomery Ward when they rejected his plan to open city stores, taking it to Sears, Roebuck, where his deduction turned out to be a gold mine, one that he enjoyed as president from 1928 to 1954.

IAN KINLOCH MACGREGOR (1912–)

A Scottish-born metallurgist, Ian MacGregor came to the U.S. during World War II, sent by the British to help in arms purchasing. He learned a lot about U.S. industry and decided to remain. He made his mark at AMAX, where he quadrupled the size of the old copper and molybdenum company by adding oil, gas, nickel, aluminum, tungsten, and iron ore to the business. Now he's back in Britain as head of the nationalized steel company.

GEORGES FEDERIC DORIOT (1899–)

One of the most popular teachers at the Harvard Business School, French-born Georges Doriot taught there for 35 years, preparing some 7,000 students for success in business. While teaching at Harvard, he headed up American Research & Development (ARD), an investment company whose mandate was to help finance fledgling outfits, especially those in high technology areas. ARD bankrolled Digital Equipment.

DAVID MACKENZIE OGILVY (1911–)

Ogilvy put the eye patch on the Hathaway shirt man, and wrote one of the most famous headlines in advertising history: "At 60 miles an hour the loudest noise in this new Rolls-Royce comes from the electric clock." He introduced Schweppes to the United States. He persuaded Eleanor Roosevelt to do a TV commercial for Good Luck margarine. He built one of the world's great advertising agencies: Ogilvy & Mather. David Ogilvy's book, *Confessions of An Advertising Man,* made the best-seller list. Ogilvy, Ogilvy's father, and Ogilvy's grandfather were all born on the same day: June 23.

WALTER ABRAHAM HAAS (1889–1979)

Married to the grandniece of Levi Strauss, Walter Haas joined his father-in-law's company after World War I and then headed the company for 30 years, laying the groundwork for the transformation of Levi Strauss & Co. from a small western seller of dry-goods to the world's largest maker of clothing. He also reinforced ethical values—care for employees, responsibility to the community—that are hallmarks of this San Francisco-based firm.

1980 Laureates

ROBERT JUSTUS KLEBERG, SR. (1853–1932)

Robert Kleberg came from a prominent family of Texas pioneers. After graduating from law school at the University of Virginia in 1981, he was retained by rancher Richard King, who owned 600,000 acres of dry wilderness Texas land called the Wild Horse Desert. King died four years later, deep in debt. Kleberg then married King's daughter and worked to build the King Ranch into an awesome stomping ground for cattle. The key problem was lack of water, and Kleberg drilled dry holes for 14 years before a powerful new rig hit an artesian well on June 6, 1899. When water bubbled to the surface, the tough-minded Kleberg wept.

CHARLES CLINTON SPAULDING (1874–1952)

One of 14 children, C. C. Spaulding spent 53 years building the largest black-owned company in the nation: North Carolina Mutual Life Insurance. He started virtually from scratch when his uncle, a Durham physician, hired him to manage an insurance association that had sprung from the black "burial societies" of the day. Spaulding was the lone employee in 1899. He hired schoolteachers and ministers to sell policies in 16 states. Later he hired a second cousin, Asa Spaulding, who became the first black actuary in the country and later the first black board member in corporate America (W. T. Grant). Today, North Carolina Mutual has assets of nearly $200 million and a staff of 1,350.

GEORGE WESTINGHOUSE (1846–1914)

George Westinghouse was one of the great American inventors—air brakes for trains, electric signals for railroads, flow-control valves for natural gas. He held 361 patents and he founded 60 companies, including the one that bears his name today—Westinghouse Electric.

JOSEPH C. WILSON (1909–1971)

Joe Wilson took xerography, copying process invented in 1938, and began investing money in it in 1947. No one else was interested. His gamble paid off, resulting in one of the great post-World War II companies: Xerox. Just about everyone who ever met Joe Wilson liked him.

FREDERICK COOLIDGE CRAWFORD (1891–   )

A folksy New Englander who had great rapport with his employees, Frederick Crawford built Cleveland's Thompson Products from a small auto-parts maker into a diversified corporate giant called TRW. His labor policies were so successful that Thompson never had a work stoppage during his tenure. Crawford stepped down in 1959, but remains an active TRW board member.

WILLIAM MILFRED BATTEN (1909–)

Giant stores tend to atrophy because they don't change with the times. Milfred Batten is credited with being the main force in getting J. C. Penney to change its ways after World War II. Elected president in 1958 after he wrote a 150-page memo critiquing the company's policies, Batten moved Penney out of small towns into shopping centers, opened stores that sold hard goods like refrigerators and TV sets, issued credit cards, and started catalog and mail order insurance operations. Batten retired in 1974 and then signed on as chairman of the New York Stock Exchange.

WILLIAM ALLAN PATTERSON (1899–1980)

"Pat" Patterson was a loan officer with Wells Fargo Bank in San Francisco in 1927 when he loaned $5,000 to help a pilot who was starting an airline on the West Coast; he then arranged the sale of that airline to Boeing; later he joined Boeing. When plane makers were separated from air carriers, Patterson emerged in Chicago as president of United Air Lines, an amalgam of four lines. He ruled United from 1934 to 1966.

DEWITT WALLACE (1899–1981) & LILA ACHESON WALLACE (1899–)

Theirs is a story right out of their own magazine. DeWitt, a World War I soldier convalescing in a French hospital, dreamed up a magazine that would condense "the best" of American magazines. In 1921, he married an enthusiastic social worker (and a child of a minister, just as he was), Lila Bell Acheson. Together they printed 5,000 copies of *Reader's Digest* in a Greenwich Village office. It went on to become the most successful magazine in the United States—indeed, in the world.

1981 Laureates

EDWIN HERBERT LAND (1909–)

Dr. Land invented the instant camera after his three-year-old daughter asked him why she couldn't see the picture he had just snapped. He also headed the company, Polaroid, that developed and refined this invention into a $1 billion business.

DONALD THOMAS REGAN (1918–)

Donald Regan went to Cambridge Latin School and Harvard, but he credits his World War II Marine Corps experience with being pivotal in giving him the courage to "do what I wanted to do." What he didn't want to do is return to Harvard law school to finish up. So he hooked up with Merrill Lynch, which was already the nation's largest stockbroker. Under Regan's prodding and leadership, it turned itself into a flourishing financial supermarket, way ahead of everyone on Wall Street. Ronald Reagan tapped him to be Treasury Secretary.

JAMES WILSON ROUSE (1914–   )

Jim Rouse started a mortgage-banking firm in 1939, and went on to become a major developer of enclosed shopping malls, which helped to decimate downtown America. Rouse wanted desperately to put his talents to work improving the quality of life in America. He secretly bought up 14,000 acres of farmland between Baltimore and Washington, D.C., and built the sparkling new town of Columbia, Maryland. Now you can see Rouse's hand in the revitalization of formerly sleazy downtown areas in cities across the country: Boston's Quincy Market, Philadelphia's Gallery at Market East, Baltimore's Harborplace, and Milwaukee's Grand Avenue, among others.

WILLIS HAVILAND CARRIER (1876–1950)

Descended from a woman hanged as a witch at Salem, Willis Carrier was the father of air conditioning, making possible the explosive growth of the Sunbelt and today's steel-and-glass skyscrapers. He air-conditioned New York's Astor Hotel in 1909. The Buffalo-based company that bears his name now belongs to United Technologies.

PIERRE SAMUEL DU PONT (1870–1945)

Pierre du Pont was one of the first to figure out how to run a great big corporation. He did it first at his family's company, Du Pont, where he had to wrest control from some lethargic cousins. He continued with General Motors, where Du Pont had become the largest stockholder, figuring that cars would be a good market for its paints.

ANDREW WILLIAM MELLON (1855–1937)

Regarded as the greatest venture capitalist in American history, Pittsburgh banker Andrew Mellon made enormous amounts of money by backing the good ideas of others: aluminum (Alcoa), abrasives (Carborundum), oil (Gulf). He was Treasury Secretary for more than ten years (1921–1932), resigning after Congressman Wright Patman began investigating him for possible conflict of interest. Herbert Hoover then named him Ambassador to Britain, where he was reprimanded by the State Department for advancing the interests of Gulf Oil in the Middle East. Before he died, Mellon donated his superb art collection and the Washington, D.C. building that housed it, creating what is now the National Gallery. (Another good idea!)

OWEN D. YOUNG (1874–1962)

Owen D. Young was one of the main architects of the highly regarded management structure of General Electric. Born on an upstate New York farm, Young became a Boston lawyer who bested GE so often enough in the courts that the company hired him as general counsel in 1912. Young chaired GE from 1922 to 1939, bringing it into the modern world. His hand-picked president during that era was engineer Gerard Swope.

1982 Laureates

JACOB HENRY SCHIFF (1847–1920)

Schiff, who came to the U.S. from Germany when he was 18 years old, became one of the premier financiers of the industrialization of America. His specialty was railroads. He financed the Pennsy, the Union Pacific, and the Northern Pacific. It was said of him that he carried "every railroad in the country, every bit of rolling stock, every foot of track, and every man connected with each line—from the president down to the last brakeman—inside his head."

ADOLPH SIMON OCHS (1858–1935)

The son of German-Jewish immigrants who settled in Tennessee, Adolph Ochs left Chattanooga in 1896 to buy the *New York Times,* then a floundering daily with a circulation of 9,000. J. P. Morgan loaned him the money ($75,000) to do it. Ochs built the *Times* into the most prestigious newspaper in the country.

CHARLES MICHAEL SCHWAB (1862–1939)

Andrew Carnegie, impressed with Schwab's command of Greek, Latin, mathematics, and music, hired him to run Carnegie Steel, paying him—back in the 1890s—more than $1 million a year. Schwab convinced J. P. Morgan to put together the U.S. Steel combine, of which Carnegie Steel was the most important component. But when he was brushed aside in the newly-formed company, Schwab left to take control of U.S. Steel's biggest rival, Bethlehem Steel.

CHARLES FRANKLIN KETTERING (1876–1958)

Kettering was a mechanical genius who, in his 30 years as head of General Motors research, came up with such crucial inventions as ethyl gasoline, Freon coolant, and high-compression car engines. He held over 140 patents, including the electric self-starter that replaced the hand crank.

CHARLES KEMMONS WILSON (1913–   )

On a motor trip to Washington, D.C., in 1951, Kemmons Wilson was outraged at the fleabag tourist courts he and his family had to stay in. A year later he opened his first Holiday Inn (named after a Bing Crosby movie) in Memphis. Now there are 1,750 Holiday Inns—and the company started by Wilson is the world's largest innkeeper.

EDWARD CROSBY JOHNSON II (1898–   )

Mutual funds are places where people who don't know how to invest their money place their cash so that it can be invested for them by professionals. Johnson, a Boston lawyer, pioneered this industry, which mushroomed after World War II, and his Fidelity complex of funds (18 of them) is still going strong under the direction of his son, Edward III.

MALCOLM PURCELL MCLEAN (1913–   )

The rise and fall of American ports in the last 25 years can be traced to Malcolm McClean, the son of a poor North Carolina tobacco farmer, who revolutionized shipping with containerized cargo. McClean sold Sea-Land to R. J. Reynolds for $160 million and started over again with U.S. Lines, a distressed competitor of Sea-Land.

HOWARD JOSEPH MORGENS (1910–   )

What can you say about someone whose career spanned the introduction of Tide detergent, Crest toothpaste, Pampers disposable diapers, Mr. Clean all-purpose cleanser, and "please don't squeeze" the Charmin toilet tissue? Howard Morgens was the head honcho at Cincinnati's Procter & Gamble from 1957 to 1974. He's one of the few chief executives who came up from the ranks of advertising, but that's not surprising for a company that consistently outadvertises everyone else in the country.

V / We'll Buy It and Put a Hotel on It

America's Biggest Mergers

BUYER	SELLER	YEAR	PRICE
Du Pont	Conoco	1981	$8.4 *billion*
U.S. Steel	Marathon Oil	1981	$6.6 *billion*
Occidental Petroleum	Cities Service	1982	$4.0 *billion*
Elf Aquitaine	Texasgulf	1981	$4.3 *billion*
Connecticut General	INA	1981	$4.2 *billion*
Shell Oil	Belridge Oil	1979	$3.7 *billion*
Fluor	St. Joe Minerals	1981	$2.7 *billion*
Kuwait Petroleum	Santa Fe International	1981	$2.5 *billion*
Freeport	McMoRan	1980	$2.3 *billion*
Sun Company	Texas Pacific Oil	1980	$2.3 *billion*
Standard Oil of Ohio	Kennecott Copper	1981	$2.1 *billion*
Kraft	Dart Industries	1981	$2.1 *billion*
General Electric	Utah International	1975	$1.9 *billion*
Allied	Bendix	1982	$1.9 *billion*
Nabisco	Standard Brands	1981	$1.8 *billion*
Southern Railway	Norfolk & Western	1980	$1.7 *billion*
Mobil Oil	Marcor	1974	$1.7 *billion*
Du Pont	Christiana	1977	$1.5 *billion*
Schering	Plough	1970	$1.4 *billion*
R. J. Reynolds	Heublein	1982	$1.3 *billion*
RCA	CIT	1979	$1.3 *billion*
Baldwin United	MGIC	1981	$1.2 *billion*
Exxon	Reliance Electric	1979	$1.2 *billion*
SmithKline	Beckman Instruments	1981	$1.0 *billion*

Source: Salomon Brothers.

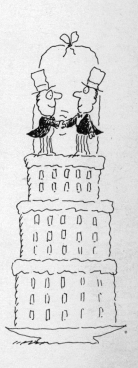

Corporate Incest

Why does Sears, Roebuck want to own 6.6% of Pinkerton's? Or is that the ultimate in store security?

More than 200 big companies own chunks of stock in 200 other companies. Here's a 1982 tally by Wall Street's Salomon Brothers of some companies owning stock in other companies:

Company A	Partly Owned by Company B	Percent Shares Held by Company B
AETNA LIFE & CASUALTY	Teledyne	5.0%
ALEXANDER'S	Interstate Properties	11.5%
ALLIED CORP	Textron	4.3%
AMAX	Standard Oil ofCalifornia	20.6%
ABC	Loews	4.8%
AMFAC	Gulf + Western	25.6%
ANALOG DEVICES	Standard Oil of Indiana	16.1%
ARMSTRONG RUBBER	Sears, Roebuck	22.4%
BANK OF NEW YORK	Gulf + Western	6.2%
BERKEY PHOTO	Transamerica	6.9%
BRUNSWICK	Gulf + Western	15.5%
BURLINGTON INDUSTRIES	Gulf + Western	4.2%
CHARTER COMPANY	American Financial	10.5%
CITY INVESTING	Sharon Steel	9.2%
	Tamco Enterprises	10.0%
CLOROX	Henkel	27.0%
COLT INDUSTRIES	Teledyne	7.7%
CUMMINS ENGINE	Gulf + Western	4.1%
DIAMOND INTERNATIONAL	Cavenham Development	33.0%
DU PONT	Seagram	20.2%
ESQUIRE	Gulf + Western	28.0%
FOUR-PHASE SYSTEMS	Corning Glass Works	3.8%
	Motorola	11.7%
	US Phillips	4.7%
GENERAL TIRE & RUBBER	Gulf + Western	24.5%
GIBRALTAR FINANCIAL	Kemper	25.0%
	Reliance Financial	7.2%
B. F. GOODRICH	Gulf + Western	9.4%
GULF + WESTERN	American Financial	7.7%
HARCOURT BRACE/JOVANOVICH	Warner Communications	8.6%
HUGHES TOOL	Borg-Warner	18.2%
INTERNATIONAL HARVESTER	Teledyne	17.0%
KELLWOOD	Sears, Roebuck	22.0%
LITTON INDUSTRIES	Teledyne	27.0%
LIBBEY-OWENS-FORD	Gulf + Western	22.7%
LOEWS	FMR	5.0%
MOHASCO	Gulf + Western	22.5%
MUNSINGWEAR	Gulf + Western	30.3%
NASHUA	Sharon Steel	10.2%
NATIONAL CONVENIENCE STORES	American Financial	21.9%
NATIONAL DISTILLERS	Panhandle Eastern	9.3%

NATIONAL STEEL	Gulf + Western	3.6%
	Hanna Mining	5.9%
NATOMAS	Signal Companies	12.5%
NEWMONT MINING	Amcon Group	22.1%
NICOR	American Brands	11.1%
NORTH AMERICAN MANUFACTURING	American Financial	83.1%
OWENS-CORNING FIBER	Corning Glass Works	23.9%
PIER 1 IMPORTS	Fuqua Industries	25.1%
PINKERTON'S*	Sears, Roebuck	6.6%
POTLATCH	Murphy Oil	6.1%
PUROLATOR	Tiger International	14.6%
RELIANCE GROUP	American Financial	12.4%
	Leasco	25.1%
REXNORD	Teledyne	6.4%
ROPER INDUSTRIES	Sears, Roebuck	41.0%
SEABOARD WORLD AIRLINES	Tiger International	24.3%
SHERWIN-WILLIAMS	Ameritrust	10.1%
	Gulf + Western	14.8%
SIMPLICITY PATTERN	Devon Group	5.5%
	Bayswater Realty	5.8%
SMITHKLINE	Fidelcor	4.2%
SOUTHWEST FOREST	Hearst	19.1%
	Reliance Financial	4.3%
STANDARD BRANDS PAINT	Sears, Roebuck	3.8%
STERNDENT	Cooper Industries	34.4%
J. P. STEVENS	Gulf + Western	15.6%
STRIDE-RITE	Textron	6.1%
TEXAS AIR	MEI	4.2%
TIGER INTERNATIONAL	Reliance Financial	19.3%
TOYS 'R' US	Petrie Stores	22.1%
TRAVELERS	Teledyne	5.3%
UNIROYAL	Gulf + Western	6.6%
UNITED FINANCIAL	National Steel	7.5%
US INDUSTRIES	Clabir	10.0%
USLIFE	American International Group	8.5%
UNITED TECHNOLOGIES	Teledyne	5.4%
WESTERN AIR LINES	Air Florida	12.6%
WHEELING PITTS STEEL	American Financial	13.4%
WM. WRIGLEY	American Home Products	9.6%
WURLITZER	Pilot Industries	10.5%

*As 1982 was drawing to a close, American Brands offered $77.50 a share to acquire Pinkerton's; the stock went into 1982 selling at $50.

A Fable of Our Times

Once upon a time there were four companies. Their names were Bendix, Martin Marietta, United Technologies, and Allied Corp. They all flourished in the second half of the 20th century.

Bendix made brakes, sparkplugs, and other parts used in automobiles and airplanes.

Martin Marietta made launch systems for the aerospace industry—it sent the Space Shuttle aloft.

United Technologies made jet engines, elevators, helicopters, air conditioners, wire, and cable.

And Allied was a chemical company that expanded into oil and gas production, batteries, electronics, and laboratory instruments.

It came to pass in 1982 that Bendix, then headed by impetuous William Agee, aided by his Harvard Business School wife, Mary Cunningham, decided that Martin Marietta would be better off as part of Bendix. It was the kind of decision Agee had been making all his business life. So he made an offer for Martin Marietta.

Now it so happened that the people at Martin Marietta were insulted by this proposal. They not only rejected it; they launched what was called a "Pac-Man defense": they made an offer to take over Bendix.

United Technologies then entered the picture. Headed by Harry Gray, United Technologies had taken over its share of companies over the previous decade; and it entered the battle on the side of Martin Marietta, making its own bid for Bendix shares.

So Bendix was asking Martin Marietta shareholders to sell their stock to Bendix. And Martin Marietta was asking Bendix shareholders to sell their stock to Martin Marietta. And they both succeeded. Well over half of the Bendix shares were offered to Martin Marietta. And well over half the Martin Marrietta shares were offered to Bendix. Thus died shareholder loyalty.

It was tantamount to a double knockout. Bendix was about to end up owning Martin Marietta, which in turned owned Bendix. Many people were reminded of old Abbott and Costello movies.

Not Edward Hennessy, though. A former Roman Catholic seminarian, Hennessy had previously worked at United Technologies, where he had watched Harry Gray consume other companies for breakfast. Having absorbed the lesson, Hennessy moved on to Allied Chemical, where as chairman he emulated Harry Gray by scooping up other companies for lunch. Taking another leaf out of the Harry Gray book, he changed the company's name. (United Technologies was formerly United Aircraft.) Hennessy dropped the "Chemical" from Allied's name to signal his appetite for nonchemical firms.

Seeing Bendix and Martin Marietta wrestle to a standstill, Hennessy plotted with Lehman Bros. and had Allied make a preemptive bid for Bendix: $1.9 billion. Agee, his back to the wall, yielded. And so, as 1982 drew to a close, Bendix breathed its last breath as an independent entity. Wtih Bendix, Allied also picked up a 39% stake in Martin Marietta (perhaps for a future meal). The shooting was over. Allied—and the merger Mafia on Wall Street—had won the war.

It was bandied about that Bill Agee might now leave the Bendix headquarters in Southfield, Michigan, near Detroit, to take a position at Hennessy's side in Morristown, New Jersey, only a short hop away from New York City, where his wife now works for Seagram. In any case, his future seemed secure. Prior to launching his missile at Martin Marietta, Agee cajoled the Bendix board into protecting him with a "golden parachute" contract that guarantees him $800,000 a year for five years in the event he is terminated.

So all's well that ends well. Many morals were drawn from this corporate Armageddon:

Economist Robert Lekachman: "four scorpions in a bottle."

The Economist: "Eating companies is wrong."

Value Line Investment Survey: "The marriage of Allied with Bendix was not made in heaven."

William Agee: "The history of American business is to a large extent a history of mergers."

The British Are Coming, the British Are Coming

Takeovers of U.S. Banks by British Banks

BARCLAYS	1968	Independent Bank, *California*
	1969	First Valley Bank, *California*
	1974	County Bank of Santa Barbara, *California*
	1974	First Westchester National Bank, *New York*
	1979	American Credit, *North Carolina*
	1980	31 Branches of Bankers Trust, *Long Island, New York*
LLOYDS	1973	First Western Bank & Trust, *California*
MIDLAND	1980	Crocker National, *California* (54% owned by Midland)
NATIONAL WESTMINSTER	1979	National Bank of North America, *New York*
STANDARD CHARTERED	1980	Union Bank, *California*

Source: *Financial Times,* July 16, 1980.

Beatrice Foods: What Big Arms You Have

Beatrice Foods started out in 1894 as a little "butter and egg" enterprise in Beatrice, Nebraska. It spent its first 50 years expanding in the dairy business, and then began to buy nondairy companies. Now headquartered at 2 North LaSalle Street in Chicago's financial canyon, Beatrice Foods, at its 88th birthday, could look across America and see, as part of its entourage, this roster of companies:

Arizona	Rosarita Mexican Foods	
California	Cal-Compack Foods	Coca-Cola Bottling of
	Del Mar Window Coverings	Los Angeles
	John Hancock Furniture	Terminal Refrigerating
	Imperial Oil & Grease	Walker Engraving
	Jordan & Horn	Wells Commercial Cooking
Colorado	Denver Cold Storage	Pepcol Manufacturing
	Electronic Processors	Samsonite (luggage)
	Jolly Rancher	
	Lowrey's Freshies	
Florida	Standard Dry Wall Products	
	Tampa Cold Storage & Warehouse	
	Tropicana Products	
Georgia	Murray Biscuit	
	South Georgia Pecan	
Idaho	C.U.I. International	
Illinois	A-1 Tool	E. R. Moore
	Accurate Threaded Fasteners	Produce Terminal Cold Storage
	Acme Die Casting	Regal Packer By-Products
	Bloomfield Industries	John Sexton
	Chicago Cold Storage	Stiffel
	Collins, Miller & Hutchings	Taylor Freezer
	Culligan International	Vogel-peterson
	E. W. Kneip	World Dryer Corp.
	Excel	Wrightway Manufacturing
	Jan & Ollier	
	Mid-West	
Indiana	ArtistOKraft (kitchen cabinets)	Peter Eckrich & Sons
	County Line Cheese	New Yorker Mobile Homes
	Cryogenic Associates	
Iowa	Vigortone Agricultural Products	

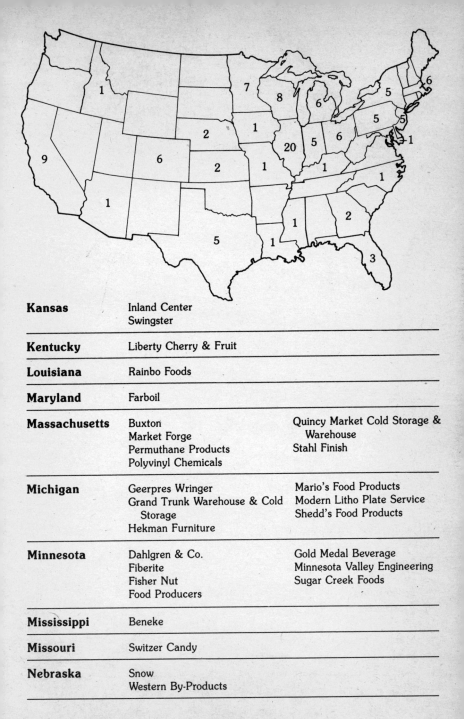

Kansas	Inland Center
	Swingster
Kentucky	Liberty Cherry & Fruit
Louisiana	Rainbo Foods
Maryland	Farboil
Massachusetts	Buxton Quincy Market Cold Storage &
	Market Forge Warehouse
	Permuthane Products Stahl Finish
	Polyvinyl Chemicals
Michigan	Geerpres Wringer Mario's Food Products
	Grand Trunk Warehouse & Cold Modern Litho Plate Service
	Storage Shedd's Food Products
	Hekman Furniture
Minnesota	Dahlgren & Co. Gold Medal Beverage
	Fiberite Minnesota Valley Engineering
	Fisher Nut Sugar Creek Foods
	Food Producers
Mississippi	Beneke
Missouri	Switzer Candy
Nebraska	Snow
	Western By-Products

New Jersey	Converters Ink	Spiegel/Bogene
	Dri-Print Foils	Webcraft Packing
	Melnor Industris	
New York	Allison Manufacturing	Harmon International Industries
	Beatrice Frosted Foods	Max H. Kahn Curtain
	Buckingham (Cutty Sark, Mouton Cadet)	Phoenix Candy
North Carolina	Krispy Kreme Doughnut	
Ohio	Beatrice Frozen Specialties	Marietta's Bakery
	Cincinnati Fruit & Extract Works	Rudolph Foods
	La Choy	Velva Sheen
Pennsylvania	D. L. Clark	Lackawanna Cold Storage
	Day Timers (mail order)	Thos. D. Richardson
	LMP	
Texas	Dearborn Brass	San Angelo By-Products
	Gebhardt Mexican Foods	Texas Tubular Products
	Lone Star Rendering	
Wisconsin	Aunt Nellie's Foods	Dell Food Specialties
	Badger By-Products	Meinerz Creamery
	Brillion Iron Works	Pfister & Vogel Tanning
	Charmglow Products (grills)	Sanna

Source: *Director of Corporate Affiliations*, published by National Register Publishing Co., Inc., Skokie, Illinois.

The Ten Most Active Corporate Acquirers

	Number of Companies Bought for More Than $1 Million in 1981
1. Gulf + Western Industries	15
2. General Electric	12
3. Reliance Group	12
4. Nucorp Energy	11
5. Pengo Industries	11
6. Alco Standard	10
7. Bass Brothers	9
8. Merrill Lynch	9
9. International Thomson Organization	8
10. National Medical Enterprises	8

Source: Reprinted with permission from *Mergers & Acquisitions*, March 24, 1982.

Most Rapacious Companies in America

Chromalloy American (bagged dozens of companies; owns 1,255 barges, 47 towboats, 12 deep-sea tankers, bus transit systems in 14 cities, clothing makers, metal fabricators—and on and on)

Gulf + Western Industries (owns Paramount Pictures, APS auto parts, Associates loan offices, Madison Square Garden, New York Rangers, Kayser-Roth, Simmons bedding, Simon & Schuster, and heavy chunks of other companies: Amfac, General Tire, Esquire, Mohasco, Munsingwear)

Hospital Corp. of America (scoops up hospitals everywhere; operated 362 hospitals with 50,969 beds as of June 30, 1982)

R. J. Reynolds Industries (Del Monte, Heublein, Chun King, College Inn, Patio, and Sea-Land now belong to this cigarette maker)

Consolidated Foods (Illinois Fruit & Vegetable, Pacific Fish, Sav-a-Stop and C&C Cola recently joined a harem that already included Sara Lee cakes, Shasta beverages, Hanes hosiery, Lawson's restaurants, Kahn's meats, Electrolux vacuum cleaners, Fuller Brush, and Douwe Egberts coffees)

Gannett (bought three daily papers and six weeklies in Mississippi during 1982 to bring its national total to 88 dailies and 32 weeklies; also started new national daily, *USA Today*)

Teledyne (owns more than 100 companies, including Water Pik, Firth Sterling, Argonaut Insurance, Packard Bell—plus 29% of Brockway Glass, 31% of Curtiss Wright, 25% of Litton, 21% of Reichhold Chemicals, 23% of Semtech, and 11% of H. J. Heinz)

American Financal (owns a dozen insurance companies and the Hunter Savings & Loan operation in Ohio, Fairmont Foods, and the Utote convenience store chain— plus 20% of Mission Insurance, 23% of National Convenience Stores, 20% of Penn Central, 20% of Gulf United, 24% of Computer Automation, 32% of United Brands, and 40% of Rapid-American)

One Big Happy Family

Consolidated Foods

Sara Lee cakes

L'eggs

Popsicles

Electrolux vacuum cleaners

Easy Come, Easy Go

Los Angeles–based Whittaker Corp. is your typical modern American corporation. It does so many things it's difficult to figure out what business it's in, save for buying and selling other companies. It makes railroad freight cars; produces cold-rolled strip steel; warehouses metal products; formulates coatings, adhesives, and sealants; owns France's largest manufacturer of hydraulic materials-handling machinery; makes the Betram, Riva, and Trojan powerboats and motor yachts, and manages health-care facilities in Saudia Arabia under such a profitable arrangement that this operation alone accounted for an estimated 75% of its profits in 1982. (Saudia Arabian investor Suliman S. Olyan happens to own 5.7% of Whittaker.)

But Whittaker's forte is clearly buying and selling. In its rise to a $1.7 billion company (triple what it was doing in 1972), Whittaker bought the following companies:

Biosystems, Inc., American Petrochemical Corp., Shock Hydrodynamics, Inc., HCl Coatings & Chemical Corp., Berwick Forge & Fabricating Corp., Fort Worth Pipe & Supply Co., Jenks Metals, Inc., Nautec Corp., Dayton Chemical Product Laboratories, Inc., Metals & Tubes, Inc., Diversified Parkway Industries, Inc., assets of Brucker Survival Capsule, Bradley & Vrooman Co., Wind Specialty Co., Inc., 1967–68; Trojan Boat Co., Kettenburg Marine Co., American Finishing Co., Electronic Resources, Inc., Yardney Electric Corp. (later changed to 76% interest), Marine Hardware Co., Production Steel Co. (Mich.), Production Steel Co. of Ill., Production Steel Strip Corp., Production Steel Coil, Inc., majority interest in Bennes Marrel S. A. 1969; Cantieri Riva S.p.A., Sarnico, Italy, TiLine, Inc., 1970; remaining 11.5% interest in Tasker Industries, 1972; remaining 14% interest in Dynasciences Corporation, 1974; Medicus Affiliates, Inc., Acrodyne Industries, 1978; CPL Corporation, a toxicological testing laboratory, Heico, Inc., Coatings and Inks Div. of M & T Chemical, Inc., Patterson-Sargent coatings plant from Textron, Inc., 1979; General Medical Corp.; The Hospital Supply-Standard Scientific div. of Ipco Corp., Great American Chemical Corp., 1980.

Meanwhile, it sold the following companies (most of which were bought originally):

Damascus Tube Co., CONSECO, Inc., Solon Industries, Inc., Crown Aluminum Industries Corp., Wesco Industries, Inc., Fanon Electronic Industries, Inc., Robien Research & Development Corp., Columbus Milpar & Mfg. Co., Inc., May Aluminum, Inc., Approved Engineering Test Laboratories, Inc., Autotec Engineering Co., Inc., ThermoPlastics Corp., Radiatronics, Inc., Royell, Inc., Nemec Industries Co., M & R Refractory Metals, Inc., Vector Co., Inc., Koppy Tool Corp., Detroit Bolt & Nut Co., Quinn Mfg. Co., Rosebrook, Inc., Irwin-Sensemich Corp., Compass Container Co., Inc., Straightline Mfg. Co., Top-Lone Products, Inc., West Coast Forge, Inc., Prime Battery Corp., Diesel Engine Sales, Inc., Western Way, Inc., Johns Technology, Inc., Diamond S. International Leasing Corp., Sommers Plastic Products Co., Inc., Athletic Sales Co., Suval Industries Inc. Masonry Products, Inc., Midwest Metal Moulding Co., Inc., S-K-S Die Casting Co., Ansen Automotive Engineer Co., Arcadia Machine & Tool Co., Eastern Foundry Supplies, Inc., Precision Forge Co., Ho-Gar Mfg. Corp., Aircraft Hydro-Forming, Inc., Bishop Tube Co., Universal Battery Co., Eden-Textiles, Inc., Kendare Corp., Rona Sea Products Corp., Rona Pearl Co., Artcraft Fabrics, Inc., Artcraft Plastics, Inc., Opco-Leather, Inc., Electronic Resources, Inc., Titanium West, Inc., Glover Co., Glover Hunt Co., net assets of Appliance Polishers, Inc., Elliott Brothers of California, Tube Polishers, Inc., Pre-Finished Metals Corp., Stainless Steel, Inc., Marcus Brothers Textile Corp., Benjamin F. Rich Co., Rich Supply Co., New Process Steel Corp., Midwest Materials, Inc., Straightline Mfg. Co., Orlite Engineering Ltd., Mercury Lithographing Corp., KniTex, Inc., Canoga Electronics Corp.; Hol-Gar and Universal Battery Divisions, 1970; Precision Forge, Philadelphia Forge, West Coast Forge, Conseco Div., Ivy Hill Lithography Corp., Turner Metals Divs., Koppy Tool Div., Courier Communications, Inc., Mercury Lithographing Corp., Rosebrook Div., 1971; Casual Furniture Manufacturing, pipeline construction operations, 1973; Marcus Brothers Textiles, Inc., Sommers Plastic Products Divs., 1976; Crown Aluminum Industries Division, 1977.

If You Can't Beat 'em, Join 'em

Beer Mergers

1966—Olympia buys out Theodore Hamm's Brewing Co.
1976—Olympia takes over Lone Star Brewery
1977—Heileman purchases Rainier
1978—Schmidt loses bid for Schaefer
1979—Heileman buys Carling National
  —Pabst acquires Blitz-Weinhard
1980—Heileman buys Duncan Brewing
1981—Stroh buys Schaefer
  —Pabst's bid for Schlitz fails
  —Schlitz agrees to merger with Heileman, but Justice Department blocks it
  —Stroh makes an offer for Schlitz
1982—Pabst bids $7.8 million for Pittsburgh Brewing
  —Pabst rejects a $131 million takeover offer from Schmidt
  —Schmidt raises bid for Pabst to $168 million
  —Stroh's bid for Schlitz is accepted
  —Olympia agrees to takeover by Pabst
  —Heileman takes over Pabst

One Big Happy Family

American Brands

Pall Mall cigarettes
Jergens lotion
Swingline staplers
Case hunting knives
Dark Eyes vodka
Titleist golf balls

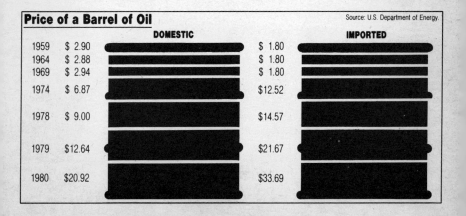

Price of a Barrel of Oil

Source: U.S. Department of Energy.

	DOMESTIC	IMPORTED
1959	$ 2.90	$ 1.80
1964	$ 2.88	$ 1.80
1969	$ 2.94	$ 1.80
1974	$ 6.87	$12.52
1978	$ 9.00	$14.57
1979	$12.64	$21.67
1980	$20.92	$33.69

Who Says Affirmative Action Doesn't Work?

In February 1966, 5.9% of all the people who worked for Sears, Roebuck were black; in December 1981, 14.6% of all Sears employees were black.

In February 1966, 2.1% of Sears employees were Hispanic; in December 1981, 6% were Hispanic.

In February 1966, 20% of the officials and managers at Sears were women; in December 1981, 38.2% were female.

The full story of what happened over those fifteen years is spelled out in the following table, which appeared in the 1981 annual report of Sears, Roebuck:

JOB CATEGORIES*	FEMALE		BLACK		HISPANIC		ASIAN/ PACIFIC ISLANDER		AMERICAN INDIAN/ ALASKAN NATIVE	
	Feb. 1966	Dec. 1981	Feb. 1966	Dec. 1981	Feb. 1966	Dec. 1981	Feb. 1966	Dec. 1981	Feb. 1966	Dec. 1981
Officials and Managers	20.0%	38.2%	0.4%	6.8%	0.7%	3.1%	0.2%	0.6%	0.1%	0.4%
Professionals	19.2%	51.4%	0.8%	8.9%	0.4%	3.6%	0.5%	1.6%	0.0%	0.1%
Technicians	48.1%	53.9%	1.1%	16.9%	0.7%	6.2%	1.5%	2.1%	0.0%	0.3%
Sales Workers	56.9%	65.3%	3.2%	12.9%	1.5%	5.4%	0.6%	1.0%	0.1%	0.3%
Office and Clerical	86.0%	85.3%	3.1%	14.1%	2.0%	6.0%	0.6%	1.2%	0.1%	0.2%
Craft Workers	3.8%	8.4%	2.8%	9.7%	2.8%	6.2%	0.7%	1.3%	0.1%	0.4%
Operatives	12.0%	13.8%	13.8%	24.4%	3.5%	8.6%	0.8%	1.0%	0.1%	0.3%
Laborers	34.3%	37.3%	18.4%	25.2%	6.5%	8.7%	0.3%	0.9%	0.1%	0.4%
Service Workers	32.3%	41.8%	44.9%	23.6%	2.0%	8.5%	0.5%	1.7%	0.1%	0.3%
All Categories	50.7%	56.4%	5.9%	14.6%	2.1%	6.0%	0.6%	1.0%	0.1%	0.3%

* Categories as defined by Equal Employment Opportunity Commission.

Where America Shops: The Top 10 General Merchandise Store Operators

	SALES	EMPLOYEES
1. **Sears, Roebuck** (*Chicago*). Has 900 stores across the U.S., sells to 24 million catalog customers.	$20.2 *billion*	337,400
2. **K mart** (*Troy, Michigan*). Has more than 2,000 stores under the K mart, Jupiter, and Kresge names; owns the Furr's cafeteria chain in the Southwest.	$16.5 *billion*	280,000
3. **J. C. Penney** (*New York*). Has some 2,000 stores across the U.S. (350 of them Thrift Drug units).	$11.8 *billion*	187,000
4. **F. W. Woolworth** (*New York*). Sales include $2.2 billion done outside the U.S., $1.1 billion from 2,800 Kinney shoe stores, and $185 million from 325 Richman's men's clothing stores.	$7.3 *billion*	139,000
5. **Federated Department Stores** (*Cincinnati*). Has 20 different department store groups, including Bloomingdale's, Abraham & Straus, Filene's, Lazarus, Bullock's and Rich's. Owns the Gold Circle discount chain and the Ralphs supermarket operation in California.	$7 *billion*	120,800
6. **Montgomery Ward** (*Chicago*). Owned by Mobil. Operates 400 stores across the U.S., trying desperately to make a comeback.	$5.7 *billion*	95,900

Tops in Slots

Biggest Corporate Croupiers
(Based on Casino Acreage)

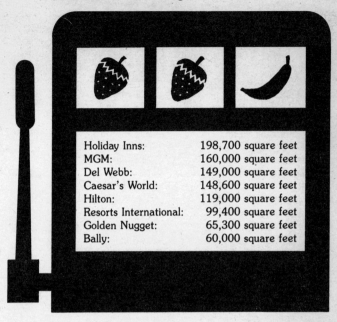

EMPLOYEES IN EACH JOB CATEGORY (in thousands)

Feb. 1966	Dec. 1981
33.4	36.9
1.3	2.9
1.5	2.5
98.7	118.2
78.6	83.0
20.8	26.9
23.4	10.7
15.2	45.8
9.9	10.4
282.8	337.4

Holiday Inns:	198,700 square feet
MGM:	160,000 square feet
Del Webb:	149,000 square feet
Caesar's World:	148,600 square feet
Hilton:	119,000 square feet
Resorts International:	99,400 square feet
Golden Nugget:	65,300 square feet
Bally:	60,000 square feet

	SALES	EMPLOYEES
7. **Household Merchandising** (*Des Plaines, Illinois*). A conglomeration of stores (furniture, hardware, food, appliance) operating under a variety of names: Von's, Ben Franklin, T.G. & Y., White. Whole shebang now owned by Household International, formerly known as Household Finance (yes, they operate the HFC small loan offices, and they also own National Car Rental).	$5 *billion*	59,900
8. **Dayton Hudson** (*Minneapolis*). Leading department store operator— Dayton's out of Minneapolis, Hudson's out of Detroit—plus discount stores, Target and Lechmere, bookstores (B. Dalton), more than 50 jewelery stores (Shreve's, Peacock's), and apparel (Mervyn's).	$4.9 *billion*	70,000
9. **May Department Stores** (*St. Louis*). Operates more than 120 department stores across the U.S. under May, Hecht, Kaufmann's, O'Neill, Meier & Frank, Famous-Barr, G. Fox, and Strouss names. Owns Venture discount stores (Kansas City, Chicago) and Volume Shoe (970 shoe stores). Also has a 23% piece of Canada's Consumer Distributing.	3.4 *billion*	68,000
10. **Carter Hawley Hale** (*Los Angeles*). Another major department store group: Broadway, Weinstock's, Emporium, Neiman-Marcus, Bergdorf-Goodman, Wanamaker, Thalhimer.	$2.8 *billion*	55,000

Where America Sleeps
The 20 Biggest Hotel Chains

		1981 Revenues	Hotels	Rooms
1.	Holiday Inns	$4.3 *billion*	1,751	308,000
2.	Sheraton (*ITT*)	$2.5 *billion*	430	113,000
3.	Best Western*	$1.9 *billion*	3,000	227,000
4.	Hilton	$1.1 *billion*	48	82,000
5.	Ramada	$1.0 *billion*	616	94,000
6.	Hyatt	$1.0 *billion*	64	36,000
7.	Westin (*United Airlines*)	$967 *million*	46	25,000
8.	Marriott	$821 *million*	115	40,000
9.	Quality Inns (*Manor Care*)	$673 *million*	494	59,000
10.	Del Webb**	$305 *million*	8	3,200
11.	Americana Hotels	$234 *million*	46	14,000
12.	Loews Hotels	$232 *million*	14	6,600
13.	Dunfey Hotels	$214 *million*	25	10,200
14.	Day Inns	$189 *million*	325	46,000
15.	Rodeway Inns	$173 *million*	151	18,000
16.	Thunderbird/Red Lion Inns	$153 *million*	47	8,800
17.	Amfac Hotels	$150 *million*	17	7,500
18.	American Motor Inns***	$142 *million*	51	7,500
19.	Stouffer (*Nestle*)	$140 *million*	22	8,000
20.	Radisson	$140 *million*	41	12,000

*Best Western is a nonprofit association; hotels are locally owned.

**You don't need a lot of hotels when you're in the gambling business. Del Webb has four hotels in Nevada, including the Saharas.

***American Motor Inns is the largest Holiday Inns franchisee.

The Ten Biggest Hotels

		Rooms	Food Sales	Alcoholic Beverages	Total Revenues
1.	Waldorf-Astoria (*New York*)	1,782	$23 *million*	$10 *million*	$87 *million*
2.	Las Vegas Hilton	3,174	$29 *million*	$18 *million*	$78 *million*
3.	Sheraton Centre (*New York*)	1,842	$12 *million*	$5 *million*	$56 *million*
4.	Disneyland Hotel (*Anaheim, California*)	1,121	$13 *million*	$4 *million*	$47 *million*
5.	Palmer House (*Chicago*)	1,900	$10 *million*	$5 *million*	$40 *million*
6.	Sheraton Boston	1,400	$9 *million*	$5 *million*	$38 *million*
7.	Innisbrook Resort (*Tarpon Springs, Florida*)	925	$9 *million*	$4 *million*	$38 *million*
8.	Hotel Del Coronado (*San Diego*)	682	$9 *million*	$3 *million*	$34 *million*
9.	Broadmoor Hotel (*Colorado Springs*)	560	$9 *million*	$4 *million*	$33 *million*
10.	San Francisco Hilton	1,167	$3 *million*	$2 *million*	$30 *million*

Source: *Restaurant Hospitality*, June 1981.

The 30 Companies with the Most Stockholders

		Number of Stockholders (early 1981)
1.	AT&T	3,026,000
2.	GENERAL MOTORS	1,191,000
3.	IBM	737,000
4.	EXXON	697,000
5.	GENERAL ELECTRIC	524,000
6.	GENERAL TELEPHONE & ELECTRONICS	486,000
7.	TEXACO	394,000
8.	SEARS, ROEBUCK	350,000
9.	FORD MOTOR	346,000
10.	SOUTHERN COMPANY	345,000
11.	AMERICAN ELECTRIC POWER	338,000
12.	GULF OIL	312,000
13.	MOBIL	272,000
14.	COMMONWEALTH EDISON	269,000
15.	PACIFIC GAS & ELECTRIC	261,000
16.	PHILADELPHIA ELECTRIC	253,000
17.	RCA	252,000
18.	U.S. STEEL	248,000
19.	STANDARD OIL OF CALIFORNIA	247,000
20.	DETROIT EDISON	242,000
21.	CONSOLIDATED EDISON	237,000
22.	EASTMAN KODAK	232,000
23.	TENNECO	232,000
24.	PUBLIC SERVICE ELECTRICITY & GAS	231,000
25.	ITT	214,000
26.	DU PONT	213,000
27.	NIAGARA MOHAWK POWER	211,000
28.	CHRYSLER CORPORATION	209,000
29.	ATLANTIC RICHFIELD	203,000
30.	NORTHEAST UTILITIES	196,000

Source: New York Stock Exchange *1981 Factbook*.

When to Speculate

October. This is one of the peculiarly dangerous months to speculate in stocks. Others are November, December, January, February, March, April, May, June, July, August and September.—*Mark Twain*

Stock Market Winners

New York Stock Exchange Companies whose stock did the best in the first ten months of 1982.

	INDUSTRY	STOCK PRICE 10/30/82	PERCENT CHANGE SINCE 12/30/81
1. Coleco Industries	toys	43.87	538
2. Bormans	grocery stores	8.25	288
3. Vendo	vending machines	7.50	253
4. Winnebago Industries	prefab houses	12.75	240
5. Mary Kay Cosmetics	cosmetics	54.37	227
6. Chrysler	auto	10.50	211
7. Limited Inc.	retail	41.25	189
8. Telex	computer equipment	18.00	177
9. Coachmen Industries	recreational vehicles	23.50	176
10. Cole National	specialty retail	40.00	170
11. Payless Cashways	retail building materials	43.50	168
12. House of Fabrics	specialty retail	29.00	167
13. Zayre	retail	58.75	145
14. Fleetwood Enterprises	prefab houses	31.50	145
15. Fabri-Centers of America	specialty retail	28.62	141
16. Lowes Companies	retail building materials	30.50	139
17. IPCO Corp.	health-care supplies	10.75	139
18. Orion Pictures	entertainment	16.00	133
19. Narco Scientific	health-care supplies	33.25	127
20. Magic Chef	appliances	20.37	126
21. A&P	grocery stores	8.75	126
22. Walgreen	drugstores	54.62	125
23. Oxford Industries	apparel	50.00	123
24. Cooper Tire & Rubber	tires	32.37	122
25. American Motors	auto	5.25	121

Source: *Forbes*, December 6, 1982.

Unbroken Quarterly Record

The following companies have paid their stockholders dividends every three months from the year indicated:

Chemical New York	1827	Cincinnati Bell	1879	Westvaco	1892
Connecticut Natural Gas	1851	Bancal Tri-State	1880	Burroughs	1985
Bay State Gas	1852	AT&T	1881	Mellon National	1985
Washington Gas Light	1852	Bell Canada	1882	Raybestos-Manhattan	1895
Irving Bank	1865	Boston Edison	1890	General Electric	1899
Travelers	1866	Commonwealth Edison	1890	Nabisco	1899
Interfirst	1875	Procter & Gamble	1891	PPG Industries	1899
Stanley Works	1877	Southern New England Telephone	1891		

Source: New York Stock Exchange *1982 Factbook*.

States with the Largest Number of Stockholders

California	4,016,000
New York	3,357,000
Illinois	1,924,000
Texas	1,898,000
Pennsylvania	1,615,000
Ohio	1,513,000
Michigan	1,385,000
Florida	1,366,000
Total	17,074,000

These eight states have more than half of the national total of 32,260,000.

States with the Smallest Number of Stockholders

Delaware	89,000
Montana	85,000
Alaska	77,000
North Dakota	71,000
South Dakota	70,000
Wyoming	70,000
Vermont	62,000

Source: New York Stock Exchange *1982 Fact Book.*

The Nation's Top 10 Law Firms

Firm Name and Principal Office	Total Number of Lawyers
1. Baker & McKenzie (*Chicago*)	622
2. Morgan, Lewis & Bockius (*Philadelphi*)	374
3. Shearman & Sterling (*New York*)	373
4. *Sidley & Austin* (*Chicago*)	348
5. Vinson & Elkins (*Houston*)	333
6. Gibson, Dunn & Crutcher (*Los Angeles*)	329
7. Fulbright & Jaworski (*Houston*)	320
8. Jones, Day, Reavis & Pogue (*Cleveland*)	317
9. Skadden, Arps, Slate, Meagher & Flom (*New York*)	306
10. Pillsbury, Madison & Sutro (*San Francisco*)	305

Source: *Legal Times of Washington,* September 1982.

Don't Tackle a Big Company Unless You Have a Lot of Money for Lawyers

Top Corporate Law Departments
(Ranked by Number of Lawyers)

	NO. OF LAWYERS	GENERAL COUNSEL	LAW SCHOOL ATTENDED
1. AT&T	924	Howard Trienens	Northwestern
2. EXXON	436	Richard S. Lombard	Harvard
3. GENERAL ELECTRIC	325	W. A. Schlotterbeck	Columbia
4. MOBIL	202	George A. Birrell	Yale
5. PRUDENTIAL	202	John B. Stoddart, Jr.	Michigan
6. STANDARD OIL OF INDIANA	201	L. B. Lea	Michigan
7. DU PONT	176	Charles E. Welch	Ohio State
8. GULF OIL	165	Jesse P. Luton, Jr.	Texas
9. SHELL OIL	158	Joseph W. Morris	Washburn
10. BANK OF AMERICA	155	George W. Coombe, Jr.	Harvard
11. GENERAL MOTORS	144	Otis M. Smith*	Catholic University
12. ATLANTIC RICHFIELD	140	F. X. McCormack	Columbia
13. IBM	138	Nicholas de B. Katzenbach**	Yale
14. SEARS, ROEBUCK	135	Philip M. Knox, Jr.	Hastings (University of California at Berkeley)
15. WESTINGHOUSE	131	Robert F. Pugliese	Georgetown
16. TENNECO	124	Walter W. Sapp	Indiana
17. RCA	116	Eugene E. Beyer, Jr.	Harvard
18. TEXACO	107	William C. Weitzel, Jr.	Harvard
19. UNION CARBIDE	106	John A. Stichnoth	Iowa
20. UNITED TECHNOLOGIES	104	Edward Large	Virginia
21. U.S. STEEL	104	Marion G. Heatwole	Washington & Lee
22. PROCTER & GAMBLE	100	Powell McHenry	Harvard
23. DOW CHEMICAL	99	I. F. Harlow	Chicago
24. ITT	98	Howard J. Aibel	Harvard
25. CONOCO	97	Andrew K. McColpin	Texas

* Otis M. Smith is the highest-ranked black in a major American corporation.

** Katzenbach was U.S. Attorney-General under President Lyndon B. Johnson. (Former general counsel for Bechtel is Caspar Weinberger, Secretary of Defense under President Ronald Reagan.)

Source: *Law and Business Directory of Corporate Counsel.*

VI / The One Place Where the U.S. Is Still Supreme (God Help Us): Advertising

Does Anyone Want to Move to Portugal?

Advertising Expenditures as Percent of Gross National Product

United States	2.02%	West Germany	1.00%
Sweden	1.88%	France	0.91%
The Netherlands	1.77%	Spain	0.89%
United Kingdom	1.74%	Luxembourg	0.60%
Switzerland	1.59%	Belgium	0.59%
Finland	1.47%	Iceland	0.51%
Norway	1.37%	Italy	0.46%
Austria	1.29%	Greece	0.33%
Denmark	1.31%	Turkey	0.31%
Ireland	1.02%	Portugal	0.20%

Reprinted with permission from *Advertising Age*, June 21, 1982.
Copyright © 1982 by Crain Communications Inc.

Vice-Presidential Mania

Advertising agency staffers are anonymous people. You never know who created that brilliant commercial you saw on TV. To make up for these wounded egos, agencies pass out a lot of vice-presidencies. Aside possibly from banking, there's no other business with so many vice-presidents. In 1981, J. Walter Thompson, the nation's second ranked agency, had on staff a total of 238 vice-presidents, 80 senior vice-presidents, 24 executive vice-presidents and two senior executive vice-presidents—and that's out of a total staff of about 3,000. Even the smaller agencies indulge in this pastime. For example, Sam Lusky Associates in Denver has 34 employees, four of them vice-presidents, three senior vice-presidents, and one executive vice-president. And Winchell Marketing Communications in Philadelphia, with a staff of 17, sports five vice-presidents. In terms of sheer numbers, banks still have the most vice-presidents. Citicorp, for example, has 2,119.

Amount of U.S. Advertising Handled	Top U.S. Ad Agencies	Some Major Clients
$1.5 billion	1. Young & Rubicam	Sanka, Jell-O, Dash, Lincoln-Mercury, Dr Pepper, 7-11, Atari, Kentucky Fried Chicken, Colony wines, Gulf Oil
$1 billion	2. J. Walter Thompson	Kodak, Ford, Kraft, Lux, Burger King, Schlitz, Quaker Oats, Harlem Globetrotters, Sears, Roebuck
$1 billion	3. Ogilvy & Mather	Maxwell House, Shake 'n Bake, Avon, Gallo, Hallmark, TWA, Contac, American Express, Shell Oil, Oakland A's
$860 million	4. Ted Bates	Bolla wines, Colgate toothpaste, Dynamo, Wonder bread, Panasonic, M&Ms, Snickers, Kal Kan, Rolaids
$858 million	5. BBDO	Pepsi-Cola, Du Pont, General Electric, Pillsbury, Gillette, Life cereal, Camel, Chicago Cubs
$838 million	6. Leo Burnett	Kellogg cereals, Marlboro, United Airlines, McDonald's, Cheer, Gleem, Oldsmobile, Allstate Insurance, RCA, Dewar's White Label Scotch
$800 million	7. Doyle Dane Bernbach	Volkswagen, Gain, Puritan oil, Polaroid, Chivas Regal, IBM, MCA, Chanel, Airwick, Mobil Oil
$794 million	8. Foote, Cone & Belding	Sara Lee, Fritos, Clairol, Kent, Levi Strauss, Sunkist, Doubleday, Zenith, Swift, Boy Scouts of America, Tahiti Tourist Board
$629 million	9. Grey Advertising	Kool-Aid, Minute Rice, Post cereals, Gordon's gin, Revlon, Bold 3, Downy, Viceroy, STP, Remington, American Motors, Renault, Massengill douches
$602 million	10. D'Arcy-MacManus & Masius	Budweiser, Milky Way, Harvey's Bristol Cream, Mazola, Thomas' English Muffins, Amoco, Cadillac, Pontiac, Whirlpool, True cigarettes, Finland National Tourist Office

Source: Reprinted with permission from *Advertising Age,* March 24, 1982. Copyright 1982 by Crain Communications.

America's Biggest Advertisers

		Advertising as percentage of sales
1. Procter & Gamble Co.	$671.8 million	5.6%
2. Sears, Roebuck & Co.	544.1 million	2.0%
3. General Foods	456.8 million	5.5%
4. Philip Morris	433.0 million	4.0%
5. General Motors	410.0 million	0.6%
6. K mart	349.6 million	2.1%
7. Nabisco Brands	341.0 million	5.9%
8. R. J. Reynolds	321.3 million	2.7%
9. AT&T	297.0 million	0.5%
10. Mobil	293.1 million	4.3%
11. Ford Motor	286.7 million	0.7%
12. Warner-Lambert	270.4 million	8.0%
13. Colgate-Palmolive	260.0 million	4.9%
14. Pepsico	260.0 million	3.7%
15. McDonald's	230.2 million	3.2%
16. American Home Products	209.0 million	5.1%
17. RCA	208.8 million	2.6%
18. J. C. Penney	208.6 million	2.1%
19. General Mills	207.3 million	3.9%
20. Bristol-Myers	200.0 million	5.7%
21. B.A.T. Industries	199.3 million	4.3%
22. Coca-Cola	197.9 million	3.4%
23. Johnson & Johnson	195.0 million	6.4%
24. Chrysler	193.0 million	1.8%
25. Ralston Purina	193.0 million	3.7%
26. U.S. Government	189.0 million	
27. Unilever	188.9 million	6.7%
28. Heublein	187.0 million	9.1%
29. Anheuser-Busch	187.2 million	4.2%
30. Dart & Kraft	177.0 million	1.7%
31. Esmark	175.0 million	5.6%
32. Gillette	171.9 million	7.4%
33. Beatrice Foods	170.0 million	1.9%

Reprinted with permission from *Advertising Age*, September 9, 1982. Copyright © 1982 by Crain Communications Inc.

The Most Expensive White Space Around

It costs more money to advertise in Parade, *a supplement distributed with Sunday newspapers, than in any other publication, newspaper or magazine. Readers pay nothing to receive* Parade, *it just comes with the Sunday paper. But it's distributed by so many papers that it can claim a total circulation of 22 million (more than any magazine)—and that's why its advertising rate is so high. If you want to place a black-and-white full-page ad in* Parade, *it will set you back $147,080; in four-color, the tab goes to $180,495.*

A Personal Service Business

The advertising agency business has been described as a "personal service business," which means that if the client takes a dislike to you, he takes his account somewhere else. It happens with thumping regularity. Account switches make news every week, and 1981 was a banner year for such movements. *Advertising Age* reported that during the year a total of $1.4 billion of advertising billings moved from one agency to another.

Among the major account switches were these:

		OLD AGENCY	NEW AGENCY
Eastern Air Lines	$54 *million*	Young & Rubicam	Campbell-Ewald
McDonald's	$53 *million*	Needham, Harper & Steers	Leo Burnett
American Airlines	$45 *million*	Doyle Dane Bernbach	Bozell & Jacobs
Pan American World Airways	$35 *million*	N. W. Ayer Doyle Dane Bernbach	Wells, Rich, Greene
Southland (7-11)	$25 *million*	J. Walter Thompson	Young & Rubicam
Republic Airlines	$20 *million*	Hoffman-York	Campbell-Mithun
STP	$17 *million*	Henderson Advertising	Grey Advertising
Hallmark Cards	$15 *million*	Foote, Cone & Belding	Young & Rubicam

Memo from Dismissed Agency: "We didn't deserve this."

Needham, Harper & Steers, the nation's 20th largest ad agency, was stunned at the end of 1981 when it was fired by the McDonald's hamburger chain. Here's the communique NH&S President Paul Harper Jr. sent to the agency's employees:

To the Organization
Subject: McDonald's: One for the Books
It hasn't happened very often; it has never happened on this scale; advertising that played a central part in the creation of a great service company.

• Bell Telephone advertising helped personalize that great company over the years and helped defend it against generations of trustbusters. But the Bell system was already there.

• Sears advertising, from the early catalogues to the television era, has shelled out product values with accuracy and drama. But it was the innovative merchandising policies of Rosenwald, Wood and their successors that made this company a national institution.

• Avis owes a lot to advertising, which brought interest and competitive edge to a routine and annoying transaction.

But to McDonald's, advertising was something different. Food is full of emotion. So are the places where people eat it.

Ray Kroc had a great idea. To a market with wildly varying standards he brought predictability; eating places where people could count on quality food and good service and cleanliness wherever they saw his sign.

But this wasn't enough. The fast food industry had a dingy image. People had to be told Ray Kroc's story. More than that, people had to be shown what the total experience of eating at McDonald's would be like.

For 10 years Needham, Harper & Steers' advertising for McDonald's was a striking and effective counterpoint between Ray Kroc's very practical values, on the one hand, and expressions of ambiance ("the McDonald's experience") on the other.

We started out with the all-time classic "You Deserve a Break Today," a campaign which raised perceptions of fast food service to the restaurant level. It became a treat instead of a mere convenience. The song, at the height of its exposure, was second only to "The Star-Spangled Banner" in popular recognition.

Our advertising for McDonald's was consistently involving. You will remember "Two-all-beef-patties-special-sauce-lettuce-cheese-pickles-onions-on-a sesame-seed bun." This became an all-family word game which swept the nation, while, at the same time, defining the product with charm and memorability.

As competition grew, it seemed wise to further personalize the advertising and the result was a second great advertising theme song, "You you're the one . . . we do it all for you."

Then later the advertising was again punctuated with a marvelous visual game, "Keep your eyes on your fries." Heavy product orientation, yes, but totally involving.

One of the many great ambiance commercials produced for McDonald's was "Mary Ryan," which, in 1979, won the Gold Lion at Cannes. It typifies the exquisite writing, casting, photography and direction which won scores of awards for McDonald's advertising over the years.

Finally, let me cite "Morning Glory" in which the relatively new McDonald's Breakfast Experience is so beautifully expressed against the music of Richie Havens. It is ironic, to say the least, that the Fast Food Industry Council voted this commercial "Best of Industry" for 1980.

This is a far from complete listing of our creative accomplishments for McDonald's. But it begins to tell you why advertising played such an important part in building McDonald's into the biggest single meal purveyor in the world.

This memorandum is not a dirge. It is a salute—a salute to a classic case of what advertising is all about.

To all of you who helped write this chapter in advertising history: Congratulations. It truly is one for the books.

God Is Like . . .

God is like Coca-Cola . . .
He's the real thing.

God is like Pan Am . . .
He makes the going great.

God is like Pepsi . . .
He's got a lot to give.

God is like VO5 hair spray . . .
He holds in all kinds of weather.

God is like Delta . . .
He's ready when you are.

God is like Frosted Flakes . . .
He's great.

God is like Hallmark . . .
He cared enough to give you the very best.

God is like Ford . . .
He has a better idea.

God is like Standard Oil . . .
You expect more.

God is like Dial soap . . .
Aren't you glad you know him?
Don't you wish everyone did?

Source: Pat Lenti, a Los Angeles businessman
(Businessmen's Law Enforcement, Northeast Los
Angeles), ran this ad in 1979 as a Christmas
message in the community paper, *Highland Park
News Herald & Journal.*

What It Costs to Buy a Page of Advertising

NEWSPAPERS:

Los Angeles Times (1 *million* circulation)	$17,100
New York Times (950,000 circulation)	$21,240
Washington Post (760,000 circulation)	$21,500
Wall Street Journal (2 *million* circulation)	$56,120

MAGAZINES:

McCall's (6.2 *million* circulation)	$65,000
Reader's Digest (18.1 *million* circulation)	$89,000
Time (5.0 *million* circulation)	$75,000
TV Guide (18.4 *million* circulation)	$76,000

Most Expensive Piece of Advertising Time

The highest price in advertising is commercial time on the Super Bowl. For the 1982 Super Bowl, advertisers were socked $350,000 per 30-second spot (in 1983, the figure was $400,000). On the other hand, considering the audience (100 million viewers), it may be one of the best buys around. Advertisers who ponied up that money in 1982 were Anheuser-Busch (Budweiser), Miller Brewing, Ford Motor, Atari, General Motors, Hertz, Subaru, and Toyota.

Radio's Golden Age of Advertising

Match the radio show with its sponsor:

Radio Show	Sponsors
1. The Jack Benny Show	A. Wheaties
2. Adventures of Superman	B. Mars Candy Co.
3. Dr. I.Q.	C. Lipton tea
4. Arthur Godfrey's Talent Scouts	D. Ovaltine
5. Sgt. Preston of the Yukon	E. Kellogg's cereals
6. Little Orphan Annie	F. Jell-O
7. The Shadow	G. Quaker puffed wheat and rice
8. Edgar Bergen and Charlie McCarthy	H. Blue Coal
9. Jack Armstrong, the All-American Boy	I. Chase and Sanborn coffee
10. The Life of Riley	J. Prell shampoo

1-F (Jack Benny/Jell-O). 2-E (Superman/Kellogg's cereals). 3-B (Dr. I.Q./Mars). 4-C (Arthur Godfrey/Lipton). 5-G (Sergeant Preston/Quaker). 6-D (Little Orphan Annie/Ovaltine). 7-H. (The Shadow/Blue Coal). 8-I (Edgar Bergen/Chase and Sanborn). 9-A (Jack Armstrong/Wheaties). 10-J (Life of Riley/Prell).

Source: Quiz by Carol Poston. Reprinted with permission from *Advertising Age*, March 8, 1982. Copyright © 1982 by Crain Communications Inc.

What's in a Face?

Can you identify the nationally known products the women or girls are associated with?

1._____

2._____

3._____

4._____

5._____

6._____

7._____

8._____

9._____

ANSWERS

1. Blue Bonnet margarine. 2. Dolly Madison bakery goods. 3. Land O' Lakes butter. 4. Creamette spaghetti. 5. Little Debbie snack cakes (McKee Baking Co.). 6. Tropicana orange juice. 7. Swiss Miss hot chocolate. 8. Morton salt. 9. Clairol Herbal Essence shampoo.

Source: *Advertising Age*, July 26, 1982.

Milestones in American Culture

Prohibitions (self-imposed) on advertising the following products on television were removed in the following sequence:

1969—feminine hygiene products

1971—hemorrhoid remedies

1972—tampons and sanitary napkins

1974—body lice cures

1976—enemas

1979—pregnancy test kits and jock-itch remedies

1980—incontinence products

1981—medicated douches

122

43 Excellent Companies

HIGH TECHNOLOGY

Allen-Bradley
Amdahl
Digital Equipment
Emerson Electric
Hewlett-Packard
IBM
Schlumberger
Texas Instruments
Data General
Hughes Aircraft
Intel
National Semiconductor
Raychem
Wang Labs

SERVICES

Delta Airlines
Marriott
McDonald's
Disney Productions
K mart
Wal-Mart

CONSUMER GOODS

Eastman Kodak
Frito-Lay (PepsiCo)
Johnson & Johnson
Procter & Gamble
Atari (Warner Comm.)
Avon
Bristol-Myers

Chesebrough-Ponds
Levi Strauss
Mars
Maytag
Merck
Revlon
Tupperware (Dart & Kraft)

RESOURCE BASED

Dow Chemical
Du Pont
Standard Oil Ind. (Amoco)

PROJECT MANAGEMENT

Bechtel
Boeing
Fluor

GENERAL INDUSTRIAL

Caterpillar Tractor
Dana Corp.
3M

Source: *In Search of Excellence*, Thomas J. Peters and Robert H. Waterman (New York: Harper & Row, 1982).

One Big Happy Family

Norton Simon

Avis Rent-A-Car
Tanqueray gin
McCall Patterns
Wesson oil

The Most Nepotistic Companies

Brown-Forman
Marriott

Leading Corporate/Private Donors to the Arts

1. Pew Charitable Trusts*	$13.1 million
2. Mobil Oil and Mobil Foundation	$12.0 million
3. Andrew W. Mellon Foundation	$11.6 million
4. Exxon	$9.0 million
5. AT&T**	$7.2 million
6. Rockefeller Foundation	$7.1 million
7. Texaco and Texaco Foundation	$5.6 million
8. Ahmanson Foundation	$5.3 million
9. Vincent Astor Foundation	$5.1 million
10. Atlantic-Richfield Foundation	$4.5 million
11. Ford Foundation	$4.0 million
12. Dayton Hudson Foundation	$3.8 million
13. Lilly Endowment	$3.5 million
14. Philip Morris	$3.3 million
15. (Amon G.) Carter Foundation	$3.1 million
16. James Irvine Foundation	$3.0 million
17. MacArthur Foundation	$2.9 million
18. Kresge Foundation	$2.8 million
19. Brown Foundation	$2.7 million
20. Gulf Oil and Gulf Oil Foundation	$2.7 million
21. IBM	$2.5 million
22. Shell Companies Foundation	$2.1 million
23. R. J. Reynolds Industries	$2.0 million
24. Moody Foundation	$2.0 million
25. United Technologies	$2.0 million

*Joseph N. Pew founded Sun Oil. Four individual government agencies spent far more for the arts than any corporation or private foundation: the National Endowment for the Arts spent $143.0 million; the National Endowment for the Humanities, $131.1 million; the New York State Council on the Arts, $35.4 million; and New York City's Department of Cultural Affairs, $28.1 million.

**Includes Bell Symphony Orchestra on tour.

Source: *In These Times*, November 3-9, 1982.

Circulation Growth of *The Wall Street Journal*

1932	1942	1946	1949	1954	1960	1966	1968	1979	1981
28,000	35,000	64,000	145,000	295,000	700,000	1,000,000	1,200,000	1,700,000	2,000,000

The Billionaires

The Richest People in America

The following dozen Americans are worth between $1 billion and $2 billion, according to *Forbes* magazine's survey of the 400 wealthiest people in the U.S. In descending order of wealth, they are:

	Hometown	Source of Wealth
Daniel Keith Ludwig	New York City	Shipping
Gordon Peter Getty	San Francisco	Getty Oil
Perry Richardson Bass	Ft. Worth	Oil, Stocks, Land
Sid Richardson Bass		
Margaret Hunt Hill	Dallas	Hunt Oil
Caroline Hunt Schoelkopf	Dallas	Hunt Oil
Philip Anschutz	Denver	Oil
Forrest Mars, Sr.	Las Vegas	M&M/Mars, Inc.
Lamar Hunt	Dallas	Hunt Oil
William Herbert Hunt	Dallas	Hunt Oil
Nelson Bunker Hunt	Dallas	Hunt Oil
David Packard	Los Altos Hills, Calif.	Hewlett-Packard
Marvin Davis	Denver	Oil

Source: *Forbes*, September 13, 1982.

The Ideal Test Markets

If you live in any of the following thirty-six cities, you're more likely to see new products than are the people living in the rest of the country. Companies are continually testing new products in small markets before foisting them on the entire population—and these, according to Advertising Age, *are the favorite "test" cities:*

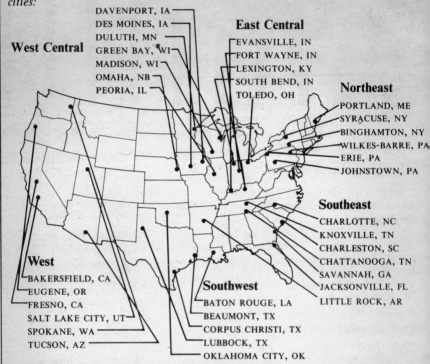

West Central
DAVENPORT, IA
DES MOINES, IA
DULUTH, MN
GREEN BAY, WI
MADISON, WI
OMAHA, NB
PEORIA, IL

East Central
EVANSVILLE, IN
FORT WAYNE, IN
LEXINGTON, KY
SOUTH BEND, IN
TOLEDO, OH

Northeast
PORTLAND, ME
SYRACUSE, NY
BINGHAMTON, NY
WILKES-BARRE, PA
ERIE, PA
JOHNSTOWN, PA

Southeast
CHARLOTTE, NC
KNOXVILLE, TN
CHARLESTON, SC
CHATTANOOGA, TN
SAVANNAH, GA
JACKSONVILLE, FL
LITTLE ROCK, AR

West
BAKERSFIELD, CA
EUGENE, OR
FRESNO, CA
SALT LAKE CITY, UT
SPOKANE, WA
TUCSON, AZ

Southwest
BATON ROUGE, LA
BEAUMONT, TX
CORPUS CHRISTI, TX
LUBBOCK, TX
OKLAHOMA CITY, OK

The Top Ten Public Relations Firms (and Their Owners)

	1981 REVENUES	EMPLOYEES
1. **Hill & Knowlton** (*J. Walter Thompson*)	$46.0 *million*	1,020
2. **Burson-Marsteller** (*Young & Rubicam*)	41.1 *million*	945
3. **Carl Byoir** (*Foote, Cone & Belding*)	18.7 *million*	454
4. **Ruder Finn & Rotman**	15.0 *million*	390
5. **Daniel J. Edelman**	8.0 *million*	170
6. **Rowland**	7.3 *million*	121
7. **Manning, Selvage & Lee** (*Benton & Bowles*)	7.1 *million*	115
8. **Ketchum**	6.0 *million*	115
9. **Doremus**	5.8 *million*	142
10. **Rogers & Cowan**	5.4 *million*	85

Source: ® J. R. O'Dwyer Co., New York.

Washington Post Says: Flacks, Keep Out

Meg Greenfield, editor of the *Washington Post's*
editorial page, sent the following memorandum to
executive editor Benjamin C. Bradlee on April 5,
1982:

*It occurs to me that I should probably share with you my thoughts on
the way the public relations firms, assorted other press agents (and, to
a certain extent, lawyers acting in behalf of their clients) are having
at us. Their attentions have multiplied enormously over the past
several months. Gray and Co., Hill & Knowlton, Byoir . . . there are
others. Governors, even members of congress, assorted other
politicians, public figures like college presidents, various lobbying
groups all have retained these firms which seem to be promising,
among their other promises, that they can get the Post to "help," can
"deliver" us in some wise.*

*Help do what? Well, promote images, sell legislation, take a stand
in support of something or other, talk about the client or, in our case
as well, receive the loved one in our editorial meeting, thereby
wasting plenty of our time.*

*If I sound a little irrational on all this it is because I am, and I have
acted on my irrationality: we have adopted a rule of simply refusing
to deal with these people—period. I have myself told some slave or
other from Hill & Knowlton that we don't traffic with press agents,
that if her client, a college president, had business to transact with us,
then the college president should call. We send back manuscripts that
come from the flacks too. I have also informed my first lawyer who
was calling, as he said, to do a little "retail business," as distinct from
calling to get us on some side of some issue from his old
governmental days, that we don't want his business, i.e., I will not
listen to him arguing the case for his independent oil dealer clients.
Like the college president, if an independent oil guy wants to call us,
let him.*

*I know this is probably inconsistent, or illogical and, like these
sweeping strictures in the past, maybe can't work. I know that it
would always be proved that if we do this, well, we should do that or
shouldn't see the other one or something, but the reason for saying no
to these wolves is plain and very strong. Why should we be in their
goddam memo traffic as exploitable or exploited "resources?" Why
should we be in their campaign plans as something "deliverable" by
their various agents who can "reach" us. Are the people at the PR
firms who say they can get the clients [an] interview, or who even say
merely they can get us on the phone for a nice working over, are they
doing anything other than selling OUR time, using US as one of their
assets? Is running a PR-firm set-up interview all that different from
running a press release:*

Anyhow, I have done this in my department, instituted the irrational Greenfield rule whose internal consistency can no doubt be demonstrated to be very weak—but which nonetheless remains our rule. We don't want any of that damned crowd around here, and if people want to get to us they need to know only 2 things: it's as easy as pie, so long as they don't come in (or send their manuscripts in or make their request) via a flack firm.

I'd like to talk about this further with all of you, if you'd like. (Sometimes, rebuffed by us, they knock on other doors—Style, for instance.) The Wall Street Journal has had a couple of very good pieces in the past couple weeks on the PR's in Washington. The guys at Newsweek, to whom I was complaining a few months ago about the onslaught say they are aware of it too. I think, as they say at Bob Jones U, we ought to smite them hip and thigh.

Bradlee replied to the memo as follows:

Meg's memo, attached, rings a bell. I recently got a letter from someone asking me to see some client of theirs, which I simply refused to answer. I will now answer it and say that we just can't go down this path.

Please be sure that all reporters and assignment editors understand what we're talking about. We will not be a party to political interviews, or really any interviews, set up by professional public relations firms. If college presidents want to talk to us they should call us, and not be charged for arranging an interview by some public relations firm.

Best Annual Reports

copious information presented clearly or dramatically

1. Amfac
2. Equitable Life
3. Foremost-McKesson
4. Gannett
5. H. J. Heinz
6. Champion International
7. E. F. Hutton
8. Lowe's Companies
9. Masco
10. Polaroid
11. R. J. Reynolds
12. Warner Communications

Worst Annual Reports

puny information indifferently presented

1. American Stores
2. American Home Products
3. Evans Products
4. Foote, Cone & Belding
5. Fuqua Industries
6. General Motors
7. General Telephone
8. Southern Pacific
9. Tenneco
10. Texaco
11. J. Walter Thompson
12. White Consolidated

The Media Conglomerates

The top 10 media companies (and their media revenues) are:

ABC	$2.3 billion
CBS	2.1 billion
RCA	1.6 billion
Time Inc.	1.5 billion
Times Mirror	1.4 billion
Gannett	1.3 billion
S. I. Newhouse	1.2 billion
Knight-Ridder	1.2 billion
Hearst	1.2 billion
Tribune Company	1.1 billion

Number 99 is Christian Science Publishing Society (Christian Science Monitor), with media revenues of $60 million, and number 100 is Stauffer Communications, Topeka, Kansas, with media revenues of $59 million from the Topeka Capital-Journal, 18 other daily papers in the Midwest, two TV stations, and seven radio stations. Stauffer also operates the Kansas City Royals Baseball Radio Network.

Source: *Advertising Age.*

ABC: Ahead of the Media Pack

The Same Company That Brought You "Charlie's Angels"
Also Brings Farmers *Hog Farm Management*

American Broadcasting Companies, New York   Total media revenues: $2.3 *billion*

ABC TELEVISION NETWORK: 207 AFFILIATES.

OWNED-AND-OPERATED TV STATIONS:

Los Angeles: KABC; San Francisco: KGO; Chicago: WLS; Detroit: WXYZ; and New York: WABC.

ABC RADIO NETWORK: 1,800 AFFILIATES.

OWNED-AND-OPERATED RADIO STATIONS:

Los Angeles: KABC-AM and KLOS-FM; San Francisco: KGO-AM and KSFX-FM; Chicago: WLS-AM and FM; Detroit: WXYZ-AM and WRIF-FM; New York: WABC-AM and WPLJ-FM; Houston: KSRR-FM; and Washington, D.C.: WRQX-FM.

CONSUMER MAGAZINES:

High Fidelity, Los Angeles, McCall's Needlework & Crafts, Modern Photography.

TRADE MAGAZINES:

Ames Group: *Industrial Distributor News, Industrial Maintenance & Plant Operations, Industrial Safety & Hygiene News, Industrial Safety Product News.*

Chilton Group: *Accent, Automotive Industries, Automotive Marketing, Chilton's Control Equipment Master, Commercial Car Journal, Distribution, Electronic Component News, Food Engineering Master, Hardware Age, Instrument & Apparatus News, Instruments & Controls Systems, Iron Age, Jewelers' Circular-Keystone, Motor Age, Product Design & Development, Review of Optometry, The Specialist, Truck & Equipment Salesman.*

Farm Progress Group: *Prairie Farmer, Wallaces Farmer, Wisconsin Agriculturist.*

Miller Group: *Dairy Herd Management, Farm Store, Merchandising, Feedlot Management, Hog Farm Management, Home & Garden Supply Merchandiser, Tack 'n' Togs.*

Hitchcock Group: *Assembly Engineering, Industrial Finishing, Infosystems, Machine & Tool Blue Book, Office Products Dealer, Quality Woodworking & Furniture Digest.*

Newspaper Graveyard

1982   134-year-old *Philadelphia Bulletin* dies

103-year-old *Cleveland Press* dies

148-year-old *Buffalo Courier-Express* dies

Minneapolis Star folds and merges into an all-day newspaper, *Minneapolis Star and Tribune*

Oakland Tribune merges into *Eastbay Today* to form *The Tribune*

Des Moines Tribune merges into *Des Moines Register*

Sarasota Journal (in Florida) merges into Sarasota *Herald-Tribune*

Portland *Oregon Journal* merges into the *Oregonian*

1981   128-year-old *Washington Star* dies

Tonight edition of the *New York Daily News* folded after one year of publishing

1980   *Allentown Chronicle* (in Pennsylvania) merges with the *Allentown Call* to become the all-day *Call-Chronicle*

Fredonia Herald (in Kansas) ceases publication

Kingsport Times (in Tennessee) merges into the morning *Kingsport News* to become the all-day *Times-News*

Madison Press Connection (in Wisconsin) dies

Monroe News-Star (in Louisiana) merges with the *Monroe World* to become the *News-Star-World*

New Orleans Times-Picayune merges with the *States-Item* to become the all-day *Times-Picayune/States-Item*

Oklahoma Journal in Oklahoma City dies

Paterson Evening News (in New Jersey) dies

Salem Capital journal (in Oregon) merges with the *Oregon Stateman* to become the *Statesman-Journal*

Tokeka Capital and *Topeka State Journal* merge to become the *Capital-Journal*

Uniontown Herald (in Pennsylvania) merges with the *Uniontown Standard* to become the all-day *Herald-Standard*

Wichita Beacon merges with the Wichita *Eagle* to become the *Eagle-Beacon*

The Most Read Newspapers in America
Top 24 U.S. Dailies

Source: *Editor & Publisher*, statistics from Audit Bureau of Circulation as of March 31 and September 30, 1982.

Newspaper	Circulation
WALL STREET JOURNAL	2,002,727
NEW YORK DAILY NEWS (m)	1,544,101
LOS ANGELES TIMES (m)	1,052,637
NEW YORK POST (e)	960,120
NEW YORK TIMES (m)	905,675
CHICAGO TRIBUNE (all day)	758,255
WASHINGTON POST (m)	726,009
CHICAGO SUN-TIMES (m)	651,579
DETROIT NEWS (all day)	642,531
DETROIT FREE PRESS (m)	631,989
PHILADELPHIA INQUIRER (m)	553,582
SAN FRANCISCO CHRONICLE (m)	530,672
LONG ISLAND NEWSDAY (e)	515,728
BOSTON GLOBE (all day)	510,978
CLEVELAND PLAIN DEALER (m)	487,672
HOUSTON CHRONICLE (e)	419,869
NEWARK STAR LEDGER (m)	416,406
MIAMI HERALD (m)	397,953
HOUSTON POST (m)	376,455
DENVER ROCKY MT. NEWS (m)	321,693
DALLAS NEWS (m)	317,279
MILWAUKEE JOURNAL (e)	307,112
KANSAS CITY TIMES (m)	290,210
LOS ANGELES HERALD EXAMINER (e)	278,009

TOTAL DAILY CIRCULATION THROUGHOUT THE U.S. IN 1981: 62,041,176

The Best and Worst Trade Papers

Best	Worst
ADVERTISING AGE	DRUG TRADE NEWS
VARIETY	EDITOR & PUBLISHER
WOMEN'S WEAR DAILY	DRUG TOPICS
PROGRESSIVE GROCER	NATIONAL REAL ESTATE INVESTOR
BROADCASTING	

Most Watched TV Programs of All Time

PROGRAM	DATE AIRED	NETWORK	PERCENT OF TV HOUSEHOLDS VIEWING*
1. DALLAS	Nov. 21, 1980	CBS	53.3%
2. ROOTS	Jan. 30, 1977	ABC	51.1%
3. GONE WITH THE WIND—PT. 1	Nov. 7, 1976	NBC	47.7%
4. GONE WITH THE WIND—PT. 2	Nov. 8, 1976	NBC	47.4%
5. SUPER BOWL XII	Jan. 15, 1978	CBS	47.2%
6. SUPER BOWL XIII	Jan. 21, 1979	NBC	47.1%
7. BOB HOPE CHRISTMAS SHOW	Jan. 15, 1970	NBC	46.6%
8. SUPER BOWL XIV	Jan. 20, 1980	CBS	46.3%
9. ROOTS	Jan. 28, 1977	ABC	45.9%
9. THE FUGITIVE	Aug. 29, 1967	ABC	45.9%
11. ROOTS	Jan. 27, 1977	ABC	45.7%
12. ED SULLIVAN	Feb. 9, 1964	CBS	45.3%
13. BOB HOPE CHRISTMAS SHOW	Jan. 14, 1971	NBC	45.0%
14. ROOTS	Jan. 25, 1977	ABC	44.8%
15. SUPER BOWL XI	Jan. 9, 1977	NBC	44.4%
15. SUPER BOWL XV	Jan. 25, 1981	NBC	44.4%
17. SUPER BOWL VI	Jan. 16, 1972	CBS	44.2%
18. ROOTS	Jan. 24, 1977	ABC	44.1%
19. BEVERLY HILLBILLIES	Jan. 8, 1964	CBS	44.0%
20. ROOTS	Jan. 26, 1977	ABC	43.8%
20. ED SULLIVAN	Feb. 16, 1964	CBS	43.8%
22. ACADEMY AWARDS	Apr. 7, 1970	ABC	43.4%
23. BEVERLY HILLBILLIES	Jan. 15, 1964	CBS	42.8%
24. SUPER BOWL VII	Jan. 14, 1973	NBC	42.7%
25. SUPER BOWL IX	Jan. 12, 1975	NBC	42.4%

Source: A. C. Nielsen Co.

The 10 Largest Trade Magazines

(Ranked by 1980 Revenues)

1. WOMEN'S WEAR DAILY — $22.6 *million*
2. COMPUTERWORLD — $21.1 *million*
3. ADVERTISING AGE — $17.5 *million*
4. ELECTRONIC NEWS — $17.2 *million*
5. OIL & GAS JOURNAL — $16.4 *million*
6. AVIATION WEEK & SPACE TECH — $16.3 *million*
7. ELECTRONICS — $15.5 *million*
8. ENGINEERING NEWS — $15.5 *million*
9. MACHINE DESIGN RECORD — $14.4 *million*
10. ELECTRONIC DESIGN — $14.4 *million*

PROGRAM	DATE AIRED	NETWORK	PERCENT OF TV HOUSEHOLDS VIEWING*
25. *BEVERLY HILLBILLIES*	Feb. 26, 1964	CBS	42.4%
27. *SUPER BOWL X*	Jan. 18, 1976	CBS	42.3%
27. *AIRPORT*	Nov. 11, 1973	ABC	42.3%
27. *LOVE STORY*	Oct. 1, 1972	ABC	42.3%
27. *CINDERELLA*	Feb. 22, 1965	CBS	42.3%
27. *ROOTS*	Jan. 29, 1977	ABC	42.3%
32. *BEVERLY HILLBILLIES*	Mar. 25, 1964	CBS	42.2%
33. *BEVERLY HILLBILLIES*	Feb. 5, 1964	CBS	42.0%
34. *BEVERLY HILLBILLIES*	Jan. 29, 1964	CBS	41.9%
35. *MISS AMERICA PAGEANT*	Sep. 9, 1961	CBS	41.8%
35. *BEVERLY HILLBILLIES*	Jan. 1, 1964	CBS	41.8%
37. *SUPER BOWL VIII*	Jan. 13, 1974	CBS	41.6%
37. *BONANZA*	Mar. 8, 1964	NBC	41.6%
39. *BEVERLY HILLBILLIES*	Jan. 22, 1964	CBS	41.5%
40. *BONANZA*	Feb. 16, 1964	NBC	41.4%
41. *ACADEMY AWARDS*	Apr. 10, 1967	ABC	42.2%
42. *BONANZA*	Feb. 9, 1964	NBC	41.0%
43. *GUNSMOKE*	Jan. 28, 1961	CBS	40.9%
44. *BONANZA*	Mar. 28, 1965	NBC	40.8%
45. *BONANZA*	Mar. 7, 1965	NBC	40.7%
45. *ALL IN THE FAMILY*	Jan. 8, 1972	CBS	40.7%
47. *ROOTS*	Jan. 23, 1977	ABC	40.5%
47. *BONANZA*	Feb. 2, 1964	NBC	40.5%
47. *BEVERLY HILLBILLIES*	May 1, 1963	CBS	40.5%
47. *GUNSMOKE*	Feb. 25, 1961	CBS	40.5%

* Based on the percentage of households with televisions, not the number of actual viewers, because many more people have television sets now than in 1960.

The Top 10 Trade Publications
(By Number of Advertising Pages)

Ad Pages Carried in 1980

1. TRAVEL AGENT	6,707
2. ELECTRONIC NEWS	6,538
3. THE BLOOD HORSE	6,097
4. OIL & GAS JOURNAL	6,093
5. WOMEN'S WEAR DAILY	5,921
6. ELECTRONIC DESIGN	5,262
7. ELECTRONICS	4,530
8. COMPUTERWORLD	4,487
9. MACHINE DESIGN	4,147
10. ADVERTISING AGE	3,761

Source: *Folio,* September 1981.

What America Reads: I

(Based on 1980 Home Subscriptions)

1.	READER'S DIGEST	16,849,086
2.	NATIONAL GEOGRAPHIC	10,557,463
3.	BETTER HOMES & GARDENS	7,350,829
4.	T.V. GUIDE	6,966,151
5.	MODERN MATURITY	6,748,925
6.	MCCALL'S	5,467,521
7.	LADIES HOME JOURNAL	4,539,054
8.	TIME	4,116,443
9.	REDBOOK	3,473,585
10.	GOOD HOUSEKEEPING	3,420,056
11.	GUIDEPOSTS	3,398,000
12.	NEWSWEEK	2,718,878
13.	DECISION	2,700,000
14.	AMERICAN LEGION	2,595,416
15.	CONSUMER REPORTS	2,452,000
16.	PREVENTION	2,389,971
17.	PLAYBOY	2,378,892
18.	SPORTS ILLUSTRATED	2,210,017
19.	U.S. NEWS & WORLD REPORT	1,992,429
20.	DAILY WORD	1,908,238
21.	SMITHSONIAN	1,896,214
22.	FIELD & STREAM	1,863,447
23.	VFW MAGAZINE	1,765,823
24.	SOUTHERN LIVING	1,697,461
25.	NATIONAL GEOGRAPHIC WORLD	1,654,031
26.	THE ELKS MAGAZINE	1,650,336
27.	POPULAR SCIENCE	1,625,740
28.	OUTDOOR LIFE	1,529,541
29.	BOY'S LIFE	1,499,682
30.	WORKBASKET	1,482,707
31.	PARENTS	1,456,741
32.	MECHANIX ILLUSTRATED	1,426,338
33.	CHANGING TIMES	1,399,619
34.	ORGANIC GARDENING	1,325,255
35.	SUNSET	1,289,671
36.	POPULAR MECHANICS	1,281,928
37.	NATION'S BUSINESS	1,268,864
38.	MOTORLAND	1,267,225
39.	COLUMBIA	1,249,455
40.	FARM JOURNAL	1,248,915
41.	HIGHLIGHTS FOR CHILDREN	1,222,793
42.	CROSSROADS	1,200,000
43.	EBONY	1,039,323
44.	TRUE STORY	1,038,767
45.	SPORT	1,037,549
46.	BON APPETIT	999,549
47.	PSYCHOLOGY TODAY	998,508

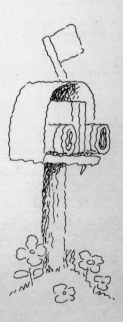

48.	THE FAMILY HANDYMAN	996,512
49.	1001 DECORATING IDEAS	993,780
50.	TRAVEL & LEISURE	950,807

The Top 50 Magazines
(Based on 1980 Newsstand Sales)

1.	T.V. GUIDE	11,460,043
2.	WOMAN'S DAY	7,626,726
3.	FAMILY CIRCLE	7,443,306
4.	NATIONAL ENQUIRER	4,540,173
5.	PENTHOUSE	4,172,454
6.	THE STAR	3,314,616
7.	PLAYBOY	2,999,926
8.	COSMOPOLITAN	2,727,930
9.	PEOPLE	1,976,708
10.	GOOD HOUSEKEEPING	1,794,835
11.	THE GLOBE	1,646,284
12.	HUSTLER	1,493,201
13.	MAD	1,263,013
14.	READER'S DIGEST	1,196,883
15.	GLAMOUR	1,152,138
16.	LADIES HOME JOURNAL	963,178
17.	MAD SPECIALS	863,500
18.	NEW WOMAN	859,778
19.	MCCALL'S NEEDLEWORK & CRAFTS	847,173
20.	REDBOOK	820,359
21.	MCCALL'S	769,655
22.	US	725,384
23.	BETTER HOMES & GARDENS	704,211
24.	SEVENTEEN	700,314
25.	MADEMOISELLE	693,386
26.	OUI	676,003
27.	OMNI	662,190
28.	VOGUE	630,784
29.	PLAYGIRL	625,177
30.	FORUM	603,359
31.	LIFE	592,268
32.	GALLERY	583,767
33.	CLUB	541,046
34.	GRIT	489,954
35.	NATIONAL LAMPOON	477,395
36.	HIGH SOCIETY	476,000
37.	SOAP OPERA DIGEST	474,382
38.	EASYRIDERS	437,177
39.	CHERI	420,475
40.	HOUSE & GARDEN	411,396
41.	POPULAR MECHANICS	404,501
42.	SELF	396,078

43. SESAME STREET	378,864
44. INSIDE SPORTS	374,450
45. TRUE STORY	362,500
46. HARPER'S BAZAAR	357,628
47. GENESIS	346,169
48. HOT ROD	344,679
49. COUNTRY LIVING	339,535
50. HIGH TIMES	321,697

Source: *Folio*, September 1981.

The Top 50 Magazines
(Based on Total Revenues in 1980)

1. T.V. GUIDE	$613,850,000
2. TIME	$346,623,000
3. READER'S DIGEST	$261,205,000
4. NEWSWEEK	$256,805,000
5. PLAYBOY	$199,279,000
6. PEOPLE	$198,502,000
7. SPORTS ILLUSTRATED	$196,183,000
8. WOMAN'S DAY	$163,455,000
9. BETTER HOMES & GARDENS	$162,909,000
10. PENTHOUSE	$162,542,000
11. FAMILY CIRCLE	$162,390,000
12. BUSINESS WEEK	$153,390,000
13. GOOD HOUSEKEEPING	$147,068,000
14. NATIONAL GEOGRAPHIC	$139,858,000
15. PARADE	$135,899,000
16. NATIONAL ENQUIRER	$124,510,000
17. U.S. NEWS & WORLD REPORT	$120,956,000
18. MCCALL'S	$120,456,000
19. LADIES HOME JOURNAL	$108,299,000
20. COSMOPOLITAN	$107,050,000
21. REDBOOK	$96,860,000
22. FAMILY WEEKLY	$88,357,000
23. THE STAR	$84,248,000
24. FORTUNE	$72,945,000
25. GLAMOUR	$63,725,000
26. FORBES	$61,228,000
27. THE NEW YORKER	$60,989,000
28. NEW YORK TIMES MAGAZINE	$56,039,000
29. HUSTLER	$54,299,000
30. SOUTHERN LIVING	$53,095,000
31. VOGUE	$52,641,000
32. LIFE	$47,025,000
33. THE GLOBE	$42,556,000
34. SMITHSONIAN	$42,522,000
35. SUNSET	$39,280,000

36.	HOUSE & GARDEN	$38,488,000
37.	NEW YORK NEWS MAGAZINE	$37,829,000
38.	SEVENTEEN	$36,939,000
39.	PREVENTION	$36,006,000
40.	POPULAR MECHANICS	$35,935,000
41.	FIELD & STREAM	$35,923,000
42.	POPULAR SCIENCE	$35,605,000
43.	EBONY	$33,120,000
44.	POPULAR PHOTOGRAPHY	$32,784,000
45.	SCIENTIFIC AMERICAN	$32,461,000
46.	MADEMOISELLE	$32,461,000
47.	CONSUMER REPORTS	$31,248,000
48.	MONEY	$30,239,000
49.	JET	$29,351,000
50.	NEW YORK	$38,832,000

Source: *Folio,* September 1981.

What American Reads: II
Books: The Bestsellers of 1981

Hardcover Fiction

		Copies Sold*
1.	NOBLE HOUSE, by James Clavell (*Delacorte*)	488,900
2.	THE HOTEL NEW HAMPSHIRE, by John Irving (*Dutton*)	372,000
3.	CUJO, by Stephen King (*Viking*)	350,000
4.	GORKY PARK, by Martin Cruz Smith (*Random House*)	273,000
5.	AN INDECENT OBSESSION, by Colleen McCullough (*Harper & Row*)	297,000
6.	MASQUERADE, by Kit Williams (*Schocken*)	245,000
7.	GOODBYE, JANETTE, by Harold Robbins (*Simon & Schuster*)	202,000
8.	THE THIRD DEADLY SIN, by Lawrence Sanders (*Putnam*)	187,400
9.	THE GLITTER DOME, by Joseph Wambaugh (*Morrow*)	180,000
10.	NO TIMES FOR TEARS, by Cynthia Freeman (*Arbor House*)	175,000
11.	GOD EMPEROR OF DUNE, by Frank Herbert (*Putnam*)	165,800

12. THE LEGACY, by Howard Fast 160,000
    (*Houghton Mifflin*)

13. THE CARDINAL SINS, by Andrew M. Greeley 143,000
    (*Warner*)

14. THE LAST DAYS OF AMERICA, by Paul Erdman 134,000
    (*Simon & Schuster*)

15. FREE FALL IN CRIMSON, John D. MacDonald 129,000
    (*Harper & Row*)

Hardcover Nonfiction

	Copies Sold*
1. THE BEVERLY HILLS DIET, by Judy Mazel (*Macmillan*)	756,300
2. THE LORD GOD MADE THEM ALL, by James Herriot (*St. Martin's*)	613,100
3. RICHARD SIMMONS' NEVER-SAY-DIET BOOK, by Richard Simmons (*Warner*)	570,000
4. A LIGHT IN THE ATTIC, by Shel Silverstein (*Harper & Row*)	544,800
5. COSMOS, by Carl Sagan (*Random House*)	487,000
6. BETTER HOMES & GARDENS NEW COOKBOOK (*Meredith*)	465,100
7. MISS PIGGY'S GUIDE TO LIFE, by Miss Piggy as told to Henry Beard (*Knopf*)	237,000
8. WEIGHT WATCHERS' 365-DAY MENU COOKBOOK (*NAL*)	230,000
9. YOU CAN NEGOTIATE ANYTHING, by Herb Cohen (*Lyle Stuart*)	205,000
10. A FEW MINUTES WITH ANDY ROONEY, by Andrew A. Rooney (*Atheneum*)	200,000
11. PATHFINDERS, by Gail Sheehy (*Morrow*)	198,000
12. HOW TO MAKE LOVE TO A MAN, by Alexandra Penney (*Clarkson N. Potter*)	196,200
13. THE WALK WEST, by Peter and Barbara Jenkins (*Morrow*)	180,000
14. ELIZABETH TAYLOR: THE LAST STAR, by Kitty Kelley (*Simon & Schuster*)	169,500
15. THE EAGLE'S GIFT, by Carlos Castaneda (*Simon & Schuster*)	169,000

*Based on publishers' own figures of copies shipped and billed.

Paperbacks

Publishers shipped 900 million paperback books in 1981. Of that number, an estimated one-third failed to sell.

The year's topselling paperbacks were:

	Copies in Print
1. THE SIMPLE SOLUTION TO RUBIK'S CUBE, by James G. Nourse (*Bantam*)	6,640,000
2. SHOGUN, by James Clavell (*Dell*)	6,600,000
3. THE COMPLETE SCARSDALE MEDICAL DIET, by Herman Tarnower and Samm Sinclair Baker (*Bantam*)	5,560,000
4. THE SHINING, by Stephen King (*NAL/Signet*)	4,500,000
5. PRINCESS DAISY, by Judith Krantz (*Bantam*)	4,000,000
6. IF THERE BE THORNS, by V. C. Andrews (*Pocket Books*)	3,830,000
7. EYE OF THE NEEDLE, by Ken Follett (*NAL/Signet*)	3,830,000
8. THE AMERICANS, by John Jakes (*Jove*)	3,815,000
9. PETALS ON THE WIND, by V. C. Andrews (*Pocket Books*)	3,713,000
10. THE FRENCH LIEUTENANT'S WOMAN, by John Fowles (*NAL/Signet*)	3,670,000

Source: Reprinted from *Publishers Weekly,* March 12, 1982, published by R. R. Bowker Company, a Xerox Company, copyright © 1982 by Xerox Corporation.

The First 10 Books Published by Pocket Books When It Went into Business in 1939

1. LOST HORIZON, by James Hilton
2. WAKE UP AND LIVE! by Dorothea Brande
3. FIVE GREAT TRAGEDIES, by William Shakespeare
4. TOPPER, by Thorne Smith
5. THE MURDER OF ROGER ACKROYD, by Agatha Christie
6. ENOUGH ROPE, by Dorothy Parker
7. WUTHERING HEIGHTS, by Emily Bronte
8. THE WAY OF ALL FLESH, by Samuel Butler
9. THE BRIDGE OF SAN LUIS REY, by Thornton Wilder
10. BAMBI, by Felix Salten

Source: Thomas Bond, *Under Cover*, (New York: Penguin, 1982).

One Big Happy Family

Figgie International
"Automatic" Sprinkler
Rawlings baseball bats
American LaFrance fire trucks

Englishmen Don't Read Magazines: The Top Ten Magazines in Britain

		Circulation
1.	WOMAN'S WEEKLY	1,487,000
2.	WOMAN'S OWN	1,401,000
3.	WOMAN	1,340,000
4.	WOMAN'S REALM	646,000
5.	FAMILY CIRCLE	621,000
6.	WOMAN & HOME	595,000
7.	WEEKEND	515,000
8.	PUZZLER	505,000
9.	LIVING	480,000
10.	COSMOPOLITAN	440,000

Source: *Economist*, July 10, 1982.

VII / So This Is the Way the World Ends

Everybody's Wired in Palm Springs

In 1982 one-third of American homes were wired to some kind of cable TV system.

The 10 Most Wired Markets in America:

1. Palm Springs, California — 100.0%
2. Santa Barbara-Santa Maria-San Luis Obispo, California — 79.2%
3. San Angelo, Texas — 76.5%
4. Laredo, Texas — 75.8%
5. Marquette, Michigan — 75.4%
6. Parkersburg, West Virginia — 73.8%
7. Casper-Riverton, Wyoming — 69.9%
8. Johnstown-Altoona, Pennsylvania — 68.8%
9. Clarksburg-Weston, West Virginia — 68.8%
10. Monterey-Salinas, California — 67.8%

The Least Wired:

1. Las Vegas, Nevada — 1%
2. Chicago, Illinois — 4%
3. Detroit, Michigan — 4%
4. Anchorage, Alaska — 5%
5. Baltimore, Maryland — 5%
6. Bowling Green, Kentucky — 5%
7. Minneapolis-St. Paul, Minnesota — 6%
8. Milwaukee, Wisconsin — 7%
9. Phoenix, Arizona — 7%
10. St. Louis, Missouri — 7%

Source: *Advertising Age,* December 7, 1981.

How About Chocolate-Covered Pickles?

Gordon McGovern, president of Campbell Soup, believes that units which don't have growth potential are candidates for expulsion. Campbell owns the nation's largest pickle packer, Vlasic, a company purchased for one million Campbell shares of stock in 1978. In 1982, McGovern told the *Wall Street Journal:*

"Packing pickle spears into glass jars is no longer good enough. I told the people at Vlasic if they couldn't see themselves as a growth company, they shouldn't be with us."

McGovern has the same story for other Campbell units: Swanson's frozen foods, Pepperidge Farms baked goods, Franco-American canned spaghetti, and Godiva chocolates.

Bank Credit Cards Now Outnumber Households

NUMBER OF CARDHOLDERS:

VISA	65 *million*
MASTERCARD	51.1 *million*

U.S. HOUSEHOLDS: 85 MILLION

PURCHASES CHARGED ON CARDS IN 1981:

VISA	$33.1 *billion*
MASTERCARD	$26.1 *billion*

MERCHANTS ACCEPTING BANK CREDIT CARDS:

VISA	1.9 *million*
MASTERCARD	2.04 *million*

Triumph of Chemistry over Nature

WORLD CONSUMPTION OF FIBERS

In the 1960–1964 period, annual world consumption of fibers broke down as follows:

Natural (cotton, wool, silk etc.): 13 million metric tons
Manmade (nylon, polyster, acrylic etc.): 4 million metric tons
                                    Total: 17 million metric tons

In 1980, world consumption broke down as follows:

Natural: 16 million metric tons
Manmade: 14 million metric tons
   Total: 30 million metric tons

Predicasts, a Cleveland-based research firm, projects 1995 consumption as follows:

Natural: 22 million metric tons
Manmade: 27 million metric tons
   Total: 49 million metric tons

Top 20 Cigarette Brands

		MARKET SHARE			MARKET SHARE
1.	Marlboro (*Philip Morris*)*	19.30%	11.	Virginia Slims (*Philip Morris*)	2.57%
2.	Winston (*R. J. Reynolds*)	13.19%	12.	Newport (*Lorillard*)	2.53%
3.	Salem (*R. J. Reynolds*)	8.77%	13.	Carlton (*American*)	2.10%
4.	Kool (*Brown & Williamson*)	7.95%	14.	More (*R. J. Reynolds*)	1.61%
5.	Benson & Hedges (*Philip Morris*)	4.91%	15.	Raleigh (*Brown & Williamson*)	1.57%
6.	Camel (*R. J. Reynolds*)	4.90%	16.	True (*Lorillard*)	1.44%
7.	Merit (*Philip Morris*)	4.48%	17.	Viceroy (*Brown & Williamson*)	1.37%
8.	Pall Mall (*American*)	4.31%	18.	Golden Lights (*Lorillard*)	1.37%
9.	Vantage (*R. J. Reynolds*)	3.87%	19.	Tareyton (*American*)	1.31%
10.	Kent (*Lorillard*)	2.79%	20.	Barclay (*Brown & Williamson*)	1.16%

Americans smoked 115 billion Marlboros in 1981.

Top 10 Liquor Brands

1960	1970	1981
Seagram's 7 Crown	Seagram's 7 Crown	Barcadi Rum
Seagram's VO	Seagram's VO	Smirnoff Vodka
Canadian Club	Canadian Club	Seagram's 7 Crown
Old Crow	Smirnoff Vodka	Seagram's VO
Walker's Imperial	J&B Rare	Jim Beam
Jim Beam	Cutty Sark	Jack Daniel's
Smirnoff Vodka	Bacardi Rum	Canadian Club
Calvert Extra	Jim Beam	Seagram's Gin
Schenley Reserve	Gordon's Gin	Popov Vodka
Early Times	Calvert Extra	Canadian Mist

Source: Impact Databank.

1981 Gambling (the Legalized Part) Revenues in the U.S.

Nevada (Las Vegas, Reno, Lake Tahoe): $2.5 billion
Atlantic City: $1.1 billion

Faster Than Bullets

Frank Resnik, president of the Tobacco Technology Group at Philip Morris, recalls that when he joined the company in 1952 as an analytical chemist, "1,250 nonfilter 70 millimeter cigarettes were produced a minute. Today, 7,200 filter cigarettes measuring 100 millimeters can be made every minute. Machine-gun bullets don't travel that fast."

One Big Happy Family

Household International

Ben Franklin variety stores
Von's supermarkets
HFC loan offices
National Car Rental
Thermos jugs

The Last of the One-Product Companies

Polaroid
Tampax
Wm. Wrigley, Jr.
Tootsie Roll Industries
Coors

Biggest Comeback of 1982

Figures are based on sales of analgesics in food stores in four U.S. cities before and after the Tylenol capsules poisoning scare of September 1982:

Brand	Prepoisoning	Wk #2	Wk #6	Wk #9
Tylenol	46.7%	6.5%	19.5%	29.9%
Anacin	15.2	29.2	22.8	17.9
Excedrin	10.1	18.8	13.5	13.6
Bufferin	9.6	17.7	14.9	13.3
Bayer	8.6	13.2	15.1	12.5

Source: *Advertising Age*, December 13, 1982.

National Health Expenditures, 1965–1981

	Total spending	Spending per person	Spending as percent of G.N.P.
1965	$ 41.7 billion	$ 211	6.0%
1966	$ 46.1 billion	$ 230	6.1%
1967	$ 53.3 billion	$ 254	6.4%
1968	$ 58.2 billion	$ 285	6.7%
1969	$ 65.6 billion	$ 318	7.0%
1970	$ 74.7 billion	$ 358	7.5%
1971	$ 83.3 billion	$ 394	7.7%
1972	$ 93.5 billion	$ 438	7.9%
1973	$ 103.2 billion	$ 478	7.8%
1974	$ 116.4 billion	$ 535	8.1%
1975	$ 132.7 billion	$ 604	8.6%
1976	$ 149.7 billion	$ 674	8.7%
1977	$ 169.2 billion	$ 755	8.8%
1978	$ 189.3 billion	$ 836	8.8%
1979	$ 215.0 billion	$ 938	8.9%
1980	$ 249.0 billion	$1,075	9.5%
1981	$ 286.6 billion	$1,225	9.8%

Source: Department of Health and Human Services.

America's Real Growth Industry: Health Care

Here are some major corporate players in the health care game:

American Medical International (*Beverly Hills, California*)

1981 sales: $913 million
Employees: 27,000
Profits: $51 million

Owns and operates 75 acute care hospitals (37 of them in California and Texas) with a total of 9,850 beds. Also operates respiratory treatment centers in 250 hospitals. Stock traded on the New York Stock Exchange.

Beverly Enterprises (*Pasadena, California*)

1981 sales: $486 million
Employees: 39,000
Profits: $16 million

Largest nursing home operator—has 494 of them (100 in Texas, 82 in California) for a total of 60,000 beds. Average occupancy (better than hotels): 88%. Stock traded on the American Stock Exchange.

Charter Medical (*Macon, Georgia*)

1981 sales: $228 million
Employees: 4,300
Profits: $12 million

Owns 17 psychiatric hospitals, 10 acute care hospitals, and one specialty surgical hospital for a total of 3,425 beds. Also operates 14 medical office buildings. Stock traded on the American Stock Exchange.

Community Psychiatric Centers (*San Francisco*)

1981 sales: $90 million
Employees: 2,900
Profits: $13 million

Operates 19 acute care psychiatric hospitals (9 of them in California). Patients stay an average of 21 days. Also has 38 kidney dialysis centers in 13 states. Stock traded on the New York Stock Exchange.

Hospital Corporation of America (*Nashville*)

1981 sales: $2 billion
Employees: 75,000
Profits: $111 million

Founded in 1968, HCA is the world's largest hospital management company. Owns or leases 362 U.S. hospitals with a total bed count of 50,969. Also owns 13 foreign hospitals with 1,530 beds. In addition, HCA manages 148 other hospital facilities. Donald S. McNaughton, former chairman of Prudential Insurance, became chairman of HCA in 1978, overseeing rapid expansion (General Care Corporation and General Health Service were acquired in 1980, Hospital Affiliates in 1981). Stock traded on the New York Stock Exchange.

Humana (*Louisville*)

1981 sales: $1.3 billion
Employees: 40,000
Profits: $93 million

Operates 88 acute care hospitals in 22 states with a total of 16,100 beds. Also runs hospitals in England and Switzerland. Stock traded on the New York Stock Exchange.

Lifemark (*Houston*)

1981 sales: $273 million
Employees: 11,260
Profits: $18 million

Owns or leases 25 general hospitals in Texas and four other states, manages 10 others under contract and provides various other services—pharmacy, physical therapy, clinical labs—to 50 more client hospitals. Also has 28 dental laboratories in 16 states. Stock traded on New York Stock Exchange.

National Medical Care (*Boston*)

1981 sales: $285 million
Employees: 5,500
Profits: $20 million

Here's the largest operator of kidney dialysis centers—it has 160 of them. NMC also operates 37 obesity control clinics. Medicare was paying $133 per dialysis treatment. When Health & Human Services Secretary Richard Schweiker announced in 1981 that the Medicare payment would be reduced to $128, NMC threatened to close 60 of its centers. The 55,000 Americans with severe kidney disease would die without these regular treatments, which cost Medicare more than $1 billion a year. NMC's stock is traded on the New York Stock Exchange.

National Medical Enterprises (*Los Angeles*)

1981 sales: $892 million
Employees: 28,200
Profits: $52 million

Operates 60 acute care hospitals and 176 nursing homes. Also distributes hospital supplies and sells telephone answering equipment. Has some drugstores. NME gets about 55% of its revenues from Medicare and Medicaid. Stock traded on the New York Stock Exchange.

One Big Happy Family

Alberto-Culver
Milani salad dressings
VO5 hair dressing
Frye boots
Sugar Twin.

Highest-Paid University Employee

Jackie Sherrill, football coach, Texas A & M, $1.7 million over six years.

The Only Graduate of Brandeis University to Head a Major Company

Christie Hefner, president, Playboy Enterprises

Companies Paying No Federal Income Taxes in 1981
Reported Profits

Company	Reported Profits
Anheuser-Busch	$217 million
Bank of America	$445 million
CSX	$367 million
Dow Chemical	$564 million
Burlington Northern	$272 million
Georgia Pacific	$160 million
John Deere	$250 million
Republic Steel	$190 million
McDonnell Douglas	$176 million
Safeway Stores	$114 million
Santa Fe Industries	$242 million
Southern Pacific	$167 million
Southern Railway	$212 million
Weyerhaeuser	$234 million
Xerox	$598 million

Source: Tax Analysts, Arlington, Virginia.

Most Unbelievable Statement of the Year

Bob Guccione, publisher of *Penthouse,* announced the formation of the Penthouse Television Network to provide cable TV operators with an adult programming service that he said would feature "tastefully selected, top-quality" programs.

The Information Society

"The restructuring of America from an industrial to an information society will easily be as profound as the shift from an agricultural society to an industrial society. But there is one important difference. While the shift from an agricultural to an industrial society took 100 years, the present restructuring from an industrial to an information society took only two decades."

—John Naisbitt in *Megatrends*

U.S.A.: Underdeveloped Country

One key indicator of underdeveloped status is tourism. When a country has more people visiting from abroad than it's sending abroad, that's a sign of underdevelopment. People elsewhere have more money to travel; they come to your country to see the sights and look for bargains. That happened to the United States in 1981 for the first time in modern history, when 23,080,203 foreigners visited the country. Meanwhile, 22,876,065 Americans traveled outside the country.

The foreign visitors spent $12.7 billion in the U.S., while Americans traveling abroad spent $11.5 billion.

One Big Happy Family

Chesebrough-Pond's

Ragu spaghetti sauce
Vaseline petroleum jelly
Prince Matchabelli perfumes

Who Produces Oil . . . and How Much Do They Have Left?

The Top 15 Oil Producers

	PERCENT OF WORLD DAILY PRODUCTION IN 1980	RESERVE LIFE**
1. U.S.S.R.	20.2%	14.3 *years*
2. Saudi Arabia	16.1%	46.9 *years*
3. United States	14.5%	8.4 *years*
4. Iraq	4.4%	31.6 *years*
5. China (P.R.C.)	3.6%	25.9 *years*
6. Venezuela	3.6%	22.9 *years*
7. Nigeria	3.5%	21.8 *years*
8. Mexico	3.3%	61.5 *years*
9. Libya	2.9%	35.4 *years*
10. United Arab Emirates	2.9%	47.9 *years*
11. United Kingdom	2.7%	25.3 *years*
12. Indonesia	2.6%	16.6 *years*
13. Canada	2.5%	11.9 *years*
14. Kuwait	2.3%	127.0 *years*
15. Iran	2.1%	123.1 *years*
TOTAL Top 15 Nations:	87.4%	29.8 *years*
WORLD TOTAL Approx. 65 producing nations:	100.0%	31.0 *years*

** Reserve life based on 1980 production rate.

Source: *Oil & Journal,* December 29, 1980.

You Think Your Gas Bills Are High?

Here are what six major airlines paid for fueling their planes in 1981:

UNITED	$1.3 *billion*
PAN AMERICAN	$1.2 *billion*
AMERICAN	$1.1 *billion*
DELTA	$1.1 *billion*
EASTERN	$1.1 *billion*
TWA	$964 *million*

Rent-A-Rig

TYPE OF UNIT	WATER DEPTH	TYPICAL DAILY RENT FOR OFFSHORE DRILLING RIGS
Marsh drilling rig	Up to 15 ft.	$6,500 to $14,000
Submersible barge	15 to 150 ft.	$15,000 to $26,000
Drill ship or semisubmersible	300 to 600+ ft.	$23,000 to $55,000

Source: *Petroleum Information Review*, 1982.

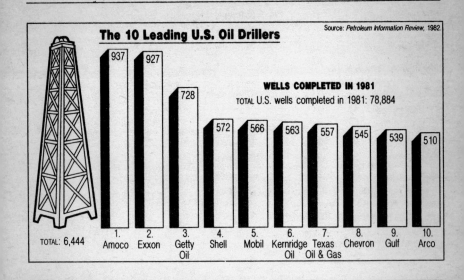

The 10 Leading U.S. Oil Drillers

Source: *Petroleum Information Review*, 1982.

WELLS COMPLETED IN 1981
TOTAL U.S. wells completed in 1981: 78,884

937 — 1. Amoco
927 — 2. Exxon
728 — 3. Getty Oil
572 — 4. Shell
566 — 5. Mobil
563 — 6. Kernridge Oil
557 — 7. Texas Oil & Gas
545 — 8. Chevron
539 — 9. Gulf
510 — 10. Arco

TOTAL: 6,444

What the Future Looks Like

—Imported cars have captured 25% of the U.S. automobile market, but their share is 50% in California.

—Among new car buyers under the age of 30, the imports have a 50% market share.

—The average age of a buyer of a U.S.–made automobile is 47; the average age of a buyer of a foreign car is 35.

—Philip Morris, second to R. J. Reynolds in the cigarette business, has a 50% market share among smokers aged 18 to 22.

—It's estimated that by the end of this century only one out of every 20 persons in the U.S. labor force will be a blue collar worker.

—Some 315,000 robots are expected to be at "work" in the U.S. by 1995, according to Predicasts, a Cleveland research organization. The U.S. robot population in 1972 was 1,000. It went over the 6,000 mark in 1981.

Who Makes the Bomb?

COMPANY	PLANT LOCATION	PRIMARY ACTIVITY	1981 CONTRACT
Bendix	Kansas City, Missouri	Produces nonnuclear components of weapons	$321 million
Du Pont	Aiken, South Carolina	Tritium separation	$560 million
General Electric	St. Petersburg, Florida	Produces a wide range of weapons components	$65 million
Mason & Hanger—Silas Mason	Amarillo, Texas	Final assembly of nuclear weapons	$74 million
Monsanto	Miamisburg, Ohio	Conducts explosives-technology research	$99 million
Rockwell International	Golden, Colorado	Produces the nuclear component of warheads	$192 million
Union Carbide	Oak Ridge, Tennessee	Fabricates and certifies nuclear weapons components	$254 million

Source: Statistics © 1982 by the New York Times Company. Reprinted by permission.

Milton Moskowitz, a longtime "corporation watcher," has been writing about business for over twenty-five years; his popular column appears in newspapers nationwide through The Los Angeles Times Syndicate.

Michael Katz is a book editor.

Robert Levering has spent eleven years writing and editing for a variety of newspapers and magazines.

Together they edited Everybody's Business: An Almanac, hailed as "a landmark!" (San Francisco Chronicle).